TWAYNE'S WORLD AUTHORS SERIES

A Survey of the World's Literature

Sylvia E. Bowman, Indiana University

GENERAL EDITOR

GREECE

John P. Anton, Emory University

EDITOR

Aristotelis Valaoritis

TWAS 406

Aristotelis Valaoritis

ARISTOTELIS
VALAORITIS

By CONSTANTINE SANTAS

Flagler College

TWAYNE PUBLISHERS

A DIVISION OF G. K. HALL & CO., BOSTON

Library of Congress Cataloging in Publication Data

Santas, Constantine.
    Aristotelis Valaoritis.

    (Twayne's world authors series ; TWAS 406 : Greece)
    Bibliography: pp. 167–70.
    Includes Index.
    1. Valaorités, Aristotelés, 1824–1879.
PA5610.B27Z88   889'.1'2   76–10673
ISBN 0–8057–6246–9

MANUFACTURED IN THE UNITED STATES OF AMERICA

To my friends from Lefkas
everywhere

Contents

About the Author

Born in Lefkas, Greece, Constantine Santas served in the Greek Army for four years and taught English to foreign students in Greece for another four years before coming to the United States to attend Knox College (Galesburg, Illinois) where he received his B.A. in 1961. In 1962 he received an M.A. in English from the University of Illinois, and in 1970 he earned his Ph.D. in American Literature from Northwestern University. Dr. Santas is presently Chairman of the English Department at Flagler College (St. Augustine, Florida), where he has taught since 1971. Previously, he has held teaching positions at the University of Illinois (Chicago Circle), and Milwaukee-Downer College.

Dr. Santas' publications include translations of Poe, Wilde, Maugham and other authors into modern Greek. He has prepared for publication a translation of Thoreau's *Walden* into modern Greek and books of translations of Greek authors including Palamas, Papadiamandis and Kondylakis. He is presently working on a forthcoming Twayne World Authors Series volume on Alexandros Papadiamandis.

Preface

Aristotelis Valaoritis is Greece's national bard, a poet uniquely suited by temperament and background for the role he played as a singer of the exploits of the fighters for freedom in the War of Independence, 1821–1828. Of a restless and passionate nature, Valaoritis spent an entire lifetime launching various battles in the political and literary arenas of Greece during the third quarter of the last century, battles that were tied together by one great purpose—to arouse the Greeks of his generation to fight on for the freedom of the still unredeemed Greek lands, Thessaly, Epirus, and Crete. Thus, the poetry of Valaoritis was clearly of patriotic content, and had a national purpose. It is poetry of power, of epic breadth, of colorful and dramatic narrations of the war of liberation, the most important stage in modern Greek history. With all its frequent rhetorical excesses—which Valaoritis inherited from the French Romantic tradition—the poetry of Valaoritis is so strongly phrased and is of such powerful utterance that it is impossible to leave a reader unmoved. For generations it has been taught to schoolchildren, who memorize it in their early days and still remember it in old age. No other poet in modern Greek history has exerted as strong and permanent an influence on the heart and imagination of the average Greek.

To the student of modern Greek literature, the study of the poetry of Valaoritis is important for several reasons. Valaoritis belongs to the Heptanesiac (Seven Islands) School of poetry, which offered the first significant literary movement in Greece, with such poets as Solomos and Kalvos as its leaders. Valaoritis, an Heptanesiac poet, moved to Athens after the union of the Heptanese with Greece in 1864, and published some of his mature poetry there. He influenced Athenian poets—namely, Achilles Paraschos, and later Kostis Palamas, the leading Greek poet of the early twentieth century. Thus, Valaoritis came to be known as a "link" between the Ionian and Athenian schools—the two most influential schools of modern Greek poetry. Another reason for studying Valaoritis is that of all the poets of his time he is the most capable linguist. He studied the spoken Greek (the demotic) for many years and used it in his poetry with accuracy—rendering its beauty in colorful descriptions of Greek nature with great dexterity. His poems—appended with glossaries and etymological explanations—are rich depositories of Greek idioms and everyday terms that provide valuable material to the student of modern Greek. Valaoritis fought throughout his life for the prevalence of the demotic with the same ardor and zeal that he exhibited in his political pursuits. Much of his poetry was, in fact, designed to demonstrate his theory that the popular language was the "living language" of Greek poetry—a language emphatically rejected by other poets and scholars of his time. Study of his poetry will reveal that, in this respect, Valaoritis accomplished his purpose perfectly.

In this study, whose disadvantage remains that it must introduce an untranslated poet to an English-speaking audience, a great deal of care has been taken to point out that Valaoritis must be studied simultaneously as a poet, a man, and a political leader. These facets of his personality interpenetrate each other and are indistinguishable. For this reason, a separate chapter has been almost totally devoted to his life and the description of his political activities. To partially solve the problem of translation, and having no aid in this respect but my own efforts, I have paraphrased in prose the plots of his major poems, hoping that their substance rather than their form has been rendered. Greek criticism on the work of Valaoritis is abundant, but hardly systematic. I have quoted the opinions of many critics where it seemed profitable to do so, and I have devoted a short last chapter to the sorting out and evaluation of the most significant of this criticism.

For the preparation of this volume many thanks are due, and I will mention persons to whom I am indebted in order. Professor Alexander Karanikas, of the University of Illinois, Chicago Circle, encouraged me to undertake this project and

Preface

helped me to find material. The late Mary Gianos was gentle, patient with my delays, and more encouraging with her letters and counsel than anyone I know. Material from Athens was sent to me by Mr. Constantine Golfinos, an almost—but not quite—forgotten friend. Professor John Anton, who took over my manuscript after the death of Mary Gianos, read it with a thoroughness and insight that has left it vastly improved. Dr. Gail Compton, of Flagler College, helped in the final editing of the manuscript with discerning corrections of style—and by typing large sections of it. I am indebted to Professor G. P. Savidis, from the University of Salonica, for kindly sending me his book on Valaoritis on short notice. Finally, I must mention my wife, Mary, who helped me track down manuscripts while she was in Athens, and who has helped me and sustained me throughout this difficult task. And a note of thanks to my father, Xenophon, who rushed to me, air mail, the last book on Valaoritis, by Mr. Gerasimos Grigoris.

CONSTANTINE SANTAS

St. Augustine, Florida
October 1975

Chronology

1824 Aristotelis Valaoritis born at Lefkas on September 1.

1838– Attends the Ionian Academy at Corfu.
1841

1841 Tours Greece accompanied by his father. Visits Athens.

1842 Travels through the northern cities of Italy.

1844 Travels to France and throughout Europe.

1846 Obtains degree from a Geneva college.

1847 *Stichourgimata* (*Verses*), his first poetry collection, is published.

1848 Obtains a doctorate in law from the University of Pisa, Italy.

1852 Marries Eloisia Typaldos in Venice.

1853 Returns to Lefkas to settle there with his wife.

1857 Elected for the first time as a deputy to the Ionian Assembly. Publishes *Mnemosyna* (*Memorial Songs*), his first major poetry collection. On July 10, he delivers his first political speech; he gains prestige and popularity as a poet and political leader.

1859 *Kyra Phrosyni*, a long narrative poem, is published.

1862 King Othon falls, after a revolution in Athens.

1863 The seven Ionian islands are united with Greece. Valaoritis recites "The Rock and the Wave," a patriotic poem, before a crowd in Corfu.

1864 Elected as the first deputy of Lefkas to the Greek National Assembly; moves to Athens.

1865 Elected again as a deputy by a large majority. Begins the composition of *Athanasis Diakos*.

1866 The Cretan Revolution breaks out in December.

1867 *Athanasis Diakos* is published in Athens.

1868 Reelected as a deputy of Lefkas to the Greek National Assembly.

1869 Gives up political career and retires to Madouri.

1872 Recites a poem dedicated to Patriarch Gregorios before a crowd in Athens. Enjoys his greatest popular triumph.

1875 Charilaos Trikoupis comes to power as prime minister. The poet's daughter, Nathalia, dies.

1877 Corresponds with Emmanuel Roidis. The Russo-Turkish war breaks out. The Treaty of San Stephano is signed.

1879 *Photeinos*, the poet's last and greatest poem, is written. Valaoritis dies on July 24, in Lefkas.

CHAPTER 1

Valaoritis and His Place in Modern Greek Literature

ARISTOTELIS Valaoritis stands in the company of Dionysios Solomos and Andreas Kalvos as one of the most influential Greek poets of the nineteenth century. Solomos (1798–1857) and Kalvos (1792–1869), writing during the generation preceding that of Valaoritis, helped reawaken the spirit of Hellenism at a time when Greeks were fighting to shake off Ottoman rule after four centuries of slavery. Solomos, in particular, became the recognized leader of the literary school of the Ionian islands, setting the standards of writing in the demotic idiom (*demotiké*), and establishing a literary tradition that was to be followed by poets of the twentieth century such as Kostis Palamas, George Seferis, and Angelos Sikelianos. Valaoritis, whose first major published collection, *Mnemosyna,* coincided with the death of Solomos, is generally regarded as a transitional figure who filled the gap between Solomos and Palamas, the leader of the Athenian School of poets. Valaoritis thus became the "link" between the Ionian and Athenian schools. But aside from this role usually assigned him, one must recognize the unique position he occupies in Greek letters: Valaoritis enjoyed immense popularity during his lifetime—a popularity still enduring in spite of the hostile attitude of some of his critics; Valaoritis contributed as much to the prevalence of the demotic in Greek poetry as any other Greek poet (certainly he contributed more than any of his contemporaries); finally, one must recognize Valaoritis not only as a national poet, a title which he shared with several others,[1] but as a writer who devoted the great bulk of his work to the description of the epic feats of the fighters for freedom during a unique period of modern Greek history, the War of Independence, 1821 to 1829.

15

I *Historical Background*

To put in its proper perspective, the poetry of Valaoritis must be seen against the background of the War of Independence and of the main events and circumstances leading to it. It is generally admitted that the decline and fall of the Byzantine Empire to the Ottoman Turks in the fifteenth century marks the beginning of the enslavement of the Greek people that was to last for four hundred years. The results of the enslavement were catastrophic in more ways than one: political leadership became extinct and cultural activity dipped to its lowest point in Greek history while the population became impoverished, suffering countless indignities. Professor C. A. Trypanis describes this period vividly:

In the centuries when the Western world was enjoying the rich fruits of the Renaissance—the fruits that had been offered by Greek learning—when in Italy, France, Spain, and England kings and bishops were the patrons of art and letters, the Greek world lay crushed under the heel of an Asiatic conqueror mercilessly extinguishing every spark of life. Its lands were devastated, its children seized and turned into Mohammedans (one-fifth of its males were for centuries collected every four years and carefully educated as Mohammedans, thus providing the sultan with a standing army and a devoted body of household slaves), its women were cast in the harems of the Muslim Pashas, its churches turned into mosques, its schools banned.[2]

By the middle of the eighteenth century, however, the Greek world had recovered somewhat from the disaster of occupation and gathered enough strength to be able to regain its freedom within a century. Of the many factors that contributed to this result, a few are worth mentioning here. Although Mohammed II, the Ottoman conqueror of Constantinople, had purged nearly all of Byzantium's political leaders, he left the Greeks a church leadership by appointing Gennadius Scholarius, a man of learning and influence, as the patriarch of Orthodox Christians. By choosing Gennadius, who had opposed reunion with Rome at the Council of Florence in 1439, Mohammed had hoped to forestall a move by western Catholic countries to come to the aid of their Christian brethren—and he proved right. Thus, the church became the spiritual (and in a sense the political) leader of the enslaved Balkan peoples and managed to preserve a form of education, however humble, in many areas.

Another factor was the rise of a merchant class among the families that clustered around the patriarchate in Constantinople. Many Greeks thus gradually rose to become a significant class, acquiring wealth and building a merchant fleet that later, during the War of Independence, would be converted into a fighting force. Greek merchants dominated the eastern Mediterranean and cultivated contacts with the West, thus opening channels of communication with more advanced cultures. Many Greeks also rose to acquire important posts in the Ottoman Empire, becoming consultants and interpreters (*dragomans*) to the sultan. Many eminent Greek families who lived in the district of Phanari (Lighthouse) in Constantinople, formed the nucleus of a social class that would later contribute members both to literary movements and to the Friendly Band (*Philiki Etaireia*), an organization that promoted the cause of Greek liberty throughout the Balkans.

Another factor was the emergence of fighters and bandits in the mountainous areas in Greece who came to be known as *armatoloi* (armed men, gendarmes) and *klephtai* (brigands, thieves)—names that were identified with the fight for freedom in the minds of the Greek people. The armatoloi were local chieftains, who frequently were appointed by Turkish authorities to maintain law and order in mountainous provinces not readily accessible to regular troops. Klephts, on the other hand, were men who, unable to endure the Ottoman rule, fled to the mountains where they established retreats (*liméria*) and from there descended on Turkish fortifications, plundering (thence the name "thief") and killing. Disenchanted armatoloi frequently became klephts, while some of the latter would occasionally obtain pardons from the sultan and turn once more into armatoloi. The lives of these men were hardy, full of adventure and peril, but they were also seen as examples of pride and heroism—and of love of freedom above all; it was this love of freedom that inspired poets to sing their legends in popular ballads. Many famous family names, such as Valaoras, Skaltsas, Vlachavas, Androutsos, Kolokotronis—to mention some of the best known—are names of klephts and armatoloi who fought before and during the War of Independence and are identified in the popular imagination with deeds of bravery that are still inspirational among Greeks.

From the middle of the eighteenth century on, there were several uprisings, especially in the Peloponnese and Epirus. In 1770 the people of the Pelopennese, stirred up by Russian agents, revolted against Turkey, but without success. Catherine the Great, whose ambition was to establish a foothold in the Balkans, attempted to stir up the Greeks to another uprising in 1786, but this time only the inhabitants of Suli, a mountainous region in Epirus, responded. Suli was destroyed by Ali Pasha, the governor of Jannina, but not without determined resistance and acts of heroism, enlisting sympathies for the cause of Greek freedom in Europe. Ali Pasha, the autocratic Albanian chieftain, had visions of himself as the Napoleon of the East and rebelled against the sultan in 1820. The latter became so preoccupied with crushing Ali's insurrection that he left the field open to the Greeks, who started the fight for their freedom with odds strongly in their favor.

The Greek War of Independence, lasting nearly eight years, is one of the glorious events of modern European history, ranking with the American and French revolutions. It led eventually to the liberation not only of the Greek people, but also of other Balkan races, such as Bulgarians, Serbians, and Rumanians, who found an opportunity to shake off the Ottoman rule once the power of the sultan had been effectively challenged by the Greeks. The great European powers—France, Russia, and England—became directly involved in the Greek struggle for freedom, while eminent men, among whom was Lord Byron, came to fight along with the Greeks (the name "philhellene"— friend of Greece—was coined at that time).

The Greeks alternated between success and failure. Initial victories—such as the capture of Tripolitza, the capital of the Peloponnese, and the destruction of the army of Pasha Mahmud Dramali in 1822—were followed by civil strife through 1823 and 1824, while some of the strongest centers of resistance,

such as the city of Missolonghi, fell back into the hands of the
Turks in 1826. Ibrahim Pasha, son of Mohammed Ali, the
sultan's vassal in Egypt, invaded the Peloponnese in June
1825, with a large army and for three years he devastated the
land, nearly extinguishing the Greek rebellion. But the great
powers intervened and saved the Greek cause by decisively
defeating the Turkish fleet at Navarino on October 20, 1827.
In 1831, after the assassination of John Kapodistrias, the first
governor of Greece, by a rival faction, the great powers again
intervened, establishing Greece as their protectorate to be
administered by Bavaria. With the Treaty of Constantinople,
May 1832, Turkey recognized Greece's independence, and on
February 6, 1833, Prince Otho, son of Louis I of Bavaria,
arrived at Nauplia to become the first king of the Hellenes—
the first king in nearly four centuries. (He later changed the
spelling of his name to "Othon," making it sound Hellenic to
please his new subjects.)

II *Literary Background*

The literary renaissance following the rebirth of the Greek
nation in the early part of the nineteenth century may be said
to have roots in three traditions. First, one may take into
account the tradition that developed in the Greek islands, many
of which either escaped Turkish domination altogether or came
to be occupied later after they had already developed significant
literatures. Cyprus and Rhodes, for instance, remained under the
rule of Venice from 1202 to 1699; Crete was not occupied by
Turkey until 1669; and the Ionian islands remained under
Venice until 1797, then under France until 1815, and under
Great Britain until 1864. The islands thus kept contacts with
the West, receiving influences that enabled them to develop
literary traditions and to keep the torch of Greek learning
aflame during the centuries of slavery. Crete, in fact, kept pace
with the literary Renaissance of Europe, and by the middle of
the seventeenth century drama and epic poetry had developed
significantly. *Erotokritos,* a long narrative poem relating the
adventures of two young lovers, is frequently cited as the
masterpiece of Cretan literature of that time. Other works were

Abraham's Sacrifice, a drama closely resembling the medieval mystery play, written by Vikentios Kornaros; and *Erophili,* a melodramatic play written by George Hortazis around 1637. The importance of Cretan poetry lies mainly in the fact that most of it was written in the demotic language, the idiom that was later to be adopted by the leaders of the Ionian School of poets—especially by Solomos—who in turn influenced the new poets of the Athenian School.

Another literary tradition developed at Phanari, in Constantinople, where a number of Greek families determinedly fostered education along with trade. The Phanariots, as they came to be called, were inspired by classical models and made it their objective to revive the ancient Greek tongue as the language befitting the literature of the young Greek nation. Indeed, they were quite determined to purify the spoken language and "to systematically avoid barbarisms."[3] The Phanariots enjoyed exceptional advantages, due mainly to their wealth and influence with the sultan, but also because of their ability to communicate with Europe and to import ideas—especially from France, whose literature influenced them most. Of their major exponents one could mention Cecarios Dapontes (1714–1784), who wrote didactic poetry using the fifteen syllable line, and was considered the greatest Greek poet of the century by his contemporaries; and Alexander Mavrokordatos (1754–1819), who wrote a great deal of poetry in the purist idiom (his *Bosporus* was published in 1810) proclaiming the superiority of a language "without impurities."[4] Many Phanariot scholars and poets moved to Athens when the liberation of Greece had been accomplished and became the leaders of the Old Athenian School. Notable among these were the brothers Alexander (1803–1863) and Panagiotis (1806–1868) Soutsos, and Alexander Rizos Rangavis (1809–1892). They all wrote patriotic poetry in the purist idiom, and one of the Soutsos brothers became famous for his satiric verse. The Phanariots were the most powerful exponents of *katharevousa* (as the purist idiom was called) and the writers most responsible for the prevalence of this idiom during the nineteenth century. In their minds, the purist language was identified with patriotism, and an author's success was to a large extent measured by his ability

to read and write classical Greek. This tendency developed
into a literary vogue (derisively called *logiotatismós* by its
opponents) that dominated Greek letters until the advent of
Palamas and his followers. The "language question"—the fight
between the advocates of the purist and those of the demotic—
is mainly an outgrowth of the firm establishment of the
Phanariots as the leading literary faction in the country by the
middle of the nineteenth century.

Folk songs (*demotiká ásmata*) provided the third strong
tradition that nourished the nineteenth century Greek literary
renaissance. Scholars usually divide Greek folk songs into
three categories (or cycles)[5]: First are the songs of human life
in its various forms and stages, including songs of love and
marriage, songs of holidays, lullabies, laments, songs expressing
grief when a beloved person leaves for a foreign land. The
second cycle consists of songs inspired by historical persons
living in a particular period of history. To this group belong
the klephtic songs, describing the life of famous klephts, their
deeds, exploits and sufferings; these songs are characterized
by a heroic pulse and have an air of heroic inspiration. Third
are the variations of these two, short narrative poems (*para-
laghes*) having in common a rapid pace; many are summaries
of tales of heroism narrated in dramatic fashion.[6]

The Greek folk songs, admired for both their simplicity and
beauty, show a people free from affectation expressing their
feelings with classical frugality. The versifier faces the natural
world with familiarity and love, often giving it human traits—
thus the frequent use of personification and a tendency to
allegorize in natural images. Mountains, for instance, talk to
one another; an eagle emblematically seeks refuge in the valley
from the heights; trees become forces of good or evil; and so
forth. Any tendency toward mysticism or introspection is absent
from Greek folk songs; the Greek seems tied with all his senses
to the external world—which he fully enjoys. Some of the songs
have a sensual character, but such sensuality is natural and
balanced, expressed within the boundaries of natural life. Death
usually means the deprivation of all goods of life and is utterly
detested. "The Christian belief in the immortality of the soul
did not penetrate into the eschatology of the popular songs,"

says Dimaras.[7] The popular song is an assertion of life and a repudiation of death.

The folk songs reached their best form around the middle of the eighteenth century, a time that saw the flowering of the· klephtic songs as the nation was preparing for its uprising. The main device of the folk song is the iambic fifteen syllable line (*decapentasýllabos*), frequently separated by a caesura, making possible a division of the line into two lines of eight and seven syllables. Thus a "ballad stanza" was formed to describe quick action. The fifteen syllable line (sometimes called *stíchos politikós*) is by and large put into closed couplets. These couplets were put to music by popular composers, or by dancers, who also improvised couplets (*madinádes*, as they are called in Crete) in response to challenges by other poets or dancers.

Of the many men who contributed to Greece's renaissance from the middle of the eighteenth century to the time of liberation, a few are worth mentioning here—men like Nikiforos Theotokis (1731–1800), Athanasios Christopoulos (1772–1847), and John Vilaras (1771–1823), collectively known as "Teachers of the Nation," who came mainly from the islands and became distinguished for both their patriotism and learning. And then there was Rhigas Pheraios (1757–1798), who was educated abroad and spent the greater part of his life studying and writing on a broad range of topics—ethics, history, science, literature, the theater. He introduced many European authors, particularly French authors, to the Greek public by translating their works. He used the spoken idiom, and wrote patriotic poetry intended to arouse Greeks everywhere to fight for their liberty. Two lines from his "Thurios" ("Paean") became famous: "For how long, oh palikars, must we live in narrow gorges, / Alone, like lions, in mountains, ravines?"[8]

Another contributor to the literary renaissance was Adamantios Korais (1748–1837), a scholar and editor of classical texts who lived most of his life abroad. Like Rhigas, Korais contributed to the liberation of Greece with his pen, attempting to define the political and literary goals of the emergent nation. "We freed the Greek lands from the Turks," he used to say, "but how many of us have freed our souls from the Turkish

else. No doubt, he had read Byron's poetry, and knew *Childe Harold* well.[12] Many of Byron's dramatic narratives—such as *The Giaour* (1813), *The Bride of Abydos* (1813), *The Corsair* (1814), and *Lara* (1814)—had become very popular and had found countless imitators throughout Europe during the first half of the nineteenth century. That Valaoritis knew these poems is attested by the composition of *Kyra Phrosyni* (1859), which imitates their style and structure. Hugo's influence on Valaoritis is perhaps more pronounced than that of any other. From Hugo, according to his own admission in a letter to Emmanuel Roidis, he inherited his "mania for contrasts," and the tendency to let his imagination "run unbridled, going wherever it wished."[13] Valaoritis had studied Hugo's works throughout his life, and once had attempted to translate his *La Lègende de siècles*, but gave up in desperation, unable to make proper names sound Greek enough.[14] The Hugoan traits in his work are grandiosity—a preference for such words as "immense," "vast," "gigantic," "terrible"—and a tendency to exaggerate, to declaim, and to be pompous or too rhetorical. Lack of control over subject matter was a trait he inherited from Hugo and other poets of the Romantic tradition. Valaoritis superceded many of these weaknesses in his mature poetry, especially that written toward the end of his life.

Valaoritis also knew quite well the works of many Romantic poets and philosophers of other European countries, particularly those of Germany and Italy. In his youth he had studied the works of Wallenstein and Schiller, as well as the critical essays of Jean Paul Richter on the poetry of his time.[15] He had translated some of the poetry of Lamartine,[16] and knew the works of Leopardi and Nicholas Tommaseo. And one cannot overlook the strong influence of Dante on Valaoritis; one of the latter's early poems describes a descent to the underworld, undoubtedly Dantean in its origin. "Thanasis Vayias," a well-known poem, contains scenes of horror and imagery clearly imitating passages of *The Inferno*.[17] Other influences on the work of Valaoritis are the Greek classical authors, particularly Pindar and Theocritus. The stylistic grandeur and tone of sublimity of some of his poems[18] owe much to Pindar, whose odes Valaoritis had studied in his youth. Theocritian elements—

detailed descriptions of nature and idyllic and pastoral scenes—
abound in his poetry. In addition, Valaoritis left translations of
several of the *Idylls* of Theocritus, apparently made very early
in his career.[19]

The significance of Valaoritis as a poet is best understood
if seen in the context of his political activities. Elected several
times (between 1854 and 1864) as a deputy to the Ionian
Assembly, and later to the Greek National Assembly, Valaoritis
spent long years and much energy trying to establish the
conditions that would allow the union of the Heptanese (and
later of Crete and other unliberated Greek lands) with Greece.
As a political leader, he was highly idealistic, incorruptible, and
unbending in his opinions, and on several occasions he refused
posts offered him by both the British Protectorate of the
Heptanese and the Greek government. As an orator, Valaoritis
was grandiloquent, enthusiastic, capable of swaying crowds to
his side, often driving them to a delirium of applause. These
traits are worth noticing, because they are often exhibited in his
poetry, where they serve identical aims. Many of his poems,
especially those written on the occasion of events of national
importance, were forceful appeals to his fellow Greeks to act
in support of national goals. Other poems aimed at reminding
Greeks of his generation of the struggles and sacrifices of the
heroic fighters of the War of Independence. In any case, both
poetry and oratory often aimed at the same target and covered
a similar trajectory. In his political speeches, and by means of
allegory in his poetry, Valaoritis stated that the Greeks of the
present generation did not equal in determination and stamina
the Greeks of the War of 1821; they must therefore be awakened
from their apathy and roused into action. To achieve this end,
poetry became in his hands a political tool, a convenient instrument.

Along with his political battles, Valaoritis fought another,
a literary one. With the publication of his first major poetry
collection, *Mnemosyna*, in 1857, he began a lifelong effort
aimed at convincing his readers and literary colleagues that the
demotic was the idiom in which Greek poetry should be written.
In this respect, Valaoritis opposed the Phanariots, who had
become entrenched in Athens by that time and had managed

to steer Greece's literary factions in the direction of archaism. He supported the theories of Solomos (whose death coincided with the publication of *Mnemosyna*) and his followers, Ioulios Typaldos, Gerasimos Markoras, and Iakovos Polylas, all of whom advocated the use of the demotic. Valaoritis was probably the most capable demoticist of his time, having mastered the Greek language in all its variations from Homer to the present. His early poetry and his political speeches show exceptional competence in the handling of *katharevousa*, though the works written in this idiom have little literary value. Valaoritis wrote his prose in the purist idiom, refuting the charge that the Heptanesiac poets wrote in the demotic because they did not know the other.[20] By writing in the *katharevousa*, he also intended to demonstrate that complete knowledge of Greek was essential for any writer.

Valaoritis' contribution to the acceptance of the demotic and his competence as a linguist are facts amply acknowledged today. "Every demotist of the present time," writes Aristos Kambanis, "is more or less a descendant of Valaoritis."[21] K. T. Dimaras, though critical of Valaoritis' rhetorical excesses, remarks that "the choice of the correct linguistic medium and the richness of his vocabulary" sets Valaoritis apart from the Athenian Romanticists, whose mournful utterances and word-hunting had degenerated into a fad.[22] Valaoritis had a healthier approach, building the idiom of his poetry from the people's speech, taking pains to learn it first-hand. His long excursions into the country, observing customs, visiting shepherds in their huts, listening to laments and songs, taking meticulous notes and compiling long glossaries which he appended to his poems, are well known.[23] He was particularly interested in the dialects of Epirus, Sterea Hellas, and Acarnania, and of course knew thoroughly the peasant idiom of Lefkas, which is richer but somewhat less euphonious and "refined" than that of the other seven islands due to Lefkas' proximity to the mainland. Valaoritis made frequent observations in his notes—some of which became prefaces to his major poems—stressing the importance and adequacy of the demotic as a means of poetic expression. Some of his theories are also to be found in his numerous letters. "The language of the people," he says in one of them,

is not impoverished but very poetic and immensely flexible. It
offers great advantages to the poet; it is self-sufficient and seldom
imitates foreign idioms. But these are small advantages compared
to the idea that the demotic is the only expression of the new
Greek poetry. It is born spontaneously, is not artificial, and is the
only branch that survives from the old trunk of our nationality.[24]

Another point that Valaoritis frequently made was that language is inseparable from national tradition and Greek history.
Language, tradition, and history are factors contributing equally
to the building of a national literature; no one factor works
in isolation from the others. The poetry of a nation, Valaoritis
claimed,[25] especially in its formative stages, must be derived
from its national tradition and historical resources, and must
of necessity be epic in character before it turns to lyric forms.
Consistent with this view, Valaoritis selected as subject matter
for his poems the recent events of the War of Independence
and its literary background. The struggles of armatoloi and
klephts against the conqueror Turk he considered the essence
of the new epic of Greece, "the fresh blood of the Greek
Parnassus, the living Greekness." The older stories of the
classical Greeks "lived only in shrouds"; the poet must, therefore, draw material for his work from what is close to his
own experience, not from what has already been written in
other literatures.[26]

IV The Poetry of Valaoritis

The poetry of Valaoritis, having its roots in the epic struggle
of a people to gain their freedom and their identity, was of
necessity poetry of action rather than of thought or introspection. He felt that no classical allusions or names should
intrude into its texture, for this would alter its tone and character. Action—tangible, immediate—is the first vital element of
the poetry of Valaoritis. The War of Independence could not
be expressed in cloudy abstractions; to make it understood
and relevant to the younger generation, the poet would have
to present the events as they happened, aiming at historical
fidelity, and using his imagination to "color" the facts rather
than subject them to his poetic convenience. The warriors of

the Revolution of 1821 were too important to be altered as characters; they could not be Manfreds, Fausts, or Rob Roys. They were the real "reformers" of Greek society, "our suffering society"; they would therefore be presented in action, during moments of struggle and sacrifice, in a manner that would inspire Greeks with their examples of patriotism. Action gives the poetry of Valaoritis its sense of immediacy. Unlike the other members of the Ionian School—Typaldos, Markoras, Kalvos, and Solomos—whose poems carry the reader to Christian, otherworldly paradises, or to the realm of Platonic ideas, Valaoritis concentrates on this world. His descriptions and images are realistic, close to life; his language "materialistic," to use the expression of Palamas.[27] Valaoritis is never lost in nebulous, foggy dreams and visions. Kalvos is Pindaric: "Solemn, sublime / Give a tone, oh lyre! / Accept the lightning / And the manner of the mind take. . . ." Solomos softens action with music: "Blood became a river, / Rolling down the ravine, / And the innocent grass drank / Blood instead of dew!" The verse of Valaoritis knits a specific course of action: "The bullet of Thanasis seeks no human flesh; / It flies straight to the horse, razes its throat. / The stallion stands up straight, in a last proud leap. . . ."

Harsh and clattering with sound, vivid in its imagery and rapid in its rhythms, the poetry of Valaoritis is rarely soft or musical; but it is often tender, as in many nature lyrics and lullabies, and some fine elegiac songs, such as the one written on the occasion of the death of his daughter Nathalia. But love affairs and romantic plots, elements so usual in the poetry of his period, are almost totally absent from his verse. Neither is Valaoritis a lyric poet. He seldom talks to or about himself, preferring the dramatic dialogue in most of his shorter poems, a device borrowed from the folk songs. In fact, most of his early poetry is nothing but "an extension and completion of the Greek folk poetry," as Palamas observes.[28] The popular muse not only inspired Valaoritis in his first poetic efforts, but also gave him his basic prosodic formula—the fifteen syllable line. Though Valaoritis used shorter lines in most of his poems of quick action, it was the fifteen syllable line that became the medium of his long narrative poems, and it was this line that

he consciously strove to perfect throughout his life. Other
devices of his poetry include the use of contrasts, a trait that,
as we have seen, he borrowed from Hugo,[29] and a habit of
presenting his subject matter in simple allegories and metaphors.
A wild vine climbing a "proud" plane tree, thus losing its
purity, or a rock demolished by a suddenly raging wave, are
images now recognized by the average Greek and have become
part of Greek folklore. Comparisons and contrasts abound: a
humble ox, ever patient and obedient to its master, suddenly
turns into a "whirlwind" of rage if stung with the goad; a little
robin, simple and peasantlike in its manners, is favorably
contrasted to a powerful but vain and foolish eagle.

Valaoritis' symbolism, unlike the symbolism of allusive or
metaphysical poetry, is facile and probably totally unconscious.
But that does not make it less meaningful. The proud mountains
frequently described in his poems are symbolic of the rugged-
ness and robustness of Greek character. They are the places
where the enslaved Greeks could breathe the air of freedom,
where they could rally against the enemy. These mountains
often became the subjects of the songs of the popular muse.
Mount Olympus, the famous abode of the ancient gods, represents the masculine element, wooing the "feminine" Mount Ossa
and begetting a famous chieftain. The Lake of Jannina, where
the beautiful Greek slave, Phrosyni, was drowned by Ali Pasha,
is the symbol of calmness and purity—Greece itself before being
violated by a conqueror. An oak tree, with its rugged strength
and longevity, can be a symbol of both good and evil. It is
a symbol of a nation that grew to gigantic proportions—the
Ottoman Empire—but that is hollow at the roots and ready
to collapse. But the tree can also shelter the rebels and give
them shade and repose when they are persecuted. The ring
worn by Athanasis Diakos, a hero who was impaled and
burned by his captors, ascends to heaven, symbolic of the
spirit that lives forever after the hero's death.

Early in his career Valaoritis had shown a tendency to
melancholy, a Byronic pensiveness, an inclination to sorrow that
contrasted vividly with the robustness and health of the other
side of his nature. This melancholy subsided during his active
years in politics, but reappeared later when deaths of members

of his family, or of friends and relatives, and disastrous national
events forced him to live in isolation at his islet, Madouri. He
then wrote many fine elegies, expressing lyrical qualities that
had been dormant in him, while his mind vacillated between
a pagan nihilism and a Christian belief in the immortality of
the soul. Death shocked and fascinated him. In his early poetry,
he viewed death in rather simplistic terms as a necessary step
in the struggle for liberty; a hero's death would inspire others
coming after him. But as bitter experience taught him other-
wise (two beloved daughters died in childhood), his view
of death gradually altered until it was conceived as a cosmic
mystery, an operation of a merciless mechanism in nature that
does not heed the existence of individuals.[30] Death is "an
invisible wheel," spinning sleeplessly. Without sentimentality,
with tragic calmness, the poet contemplates this fact:

> The nightingale, the wild flower, the rock,
> The angel face of your beloved Andonis,
> All are held by the same hand....[31]

Spending his last years in tormented anguish, but developing
a stoic strength of mind that allowed him to maintain an
affirmative view of life, Valaoritis composed poetry marked both
by the maturing of his technique and by increasing philosophical
depth. His masterpiece, *Photeinos* (1879), expresses his complete knowledge of the popular idiom, his intimate familiarity
with Greek nature, his love of country finally transmuted into
the love of the ideal and of man, and his coming to terms with
the fact of death. All these factors contributed to the composition
of an almost flawless poem of three cantos—a poem admired
even by the most difficult of his critics.

CHAPTER 2

Valaoritis: His Life and Times

IN his biographical note on Valaoritis, Marquis de Queux de St. Hilaire wrote:

Aristotelis Valaoritis was a true poet, and by the same token a true patriot. He was Greece's national poet, the popular singer of the glorious and mournful pages of her modern history, the passionate spokesman of her sorrows and desires. One can say about him that the heart of his country beat in his chest. His poems, written in the popular tongue, were the last echo of the klephtic songs, which reverberated in the mountains of Epirus.[1]

According to John Valaoritis, son of the poet, the above statement is a summary of the poet's life. A biographer, he continues,

ought to present the poet's life as a noble and harmonious whole, centering on this one point: the poet's boundless and warm-hearted love for his country. Never did the slightest cloud shadow his soul's luminous clarity—nor could the greatest setback shake the integrity of his character. To this love he devoted his entire life, health, property, and individual interests, giving lavishly, never asking, frequently turning down positions, honors, which at any rate would be rightfully his.[2]

I Early Life and Travels

The ancestors of the family of Aristotelis Valaoritis came from Valaora, a small town in Euritania, near the Acheloos River, in the province of Epirus. Many of his forefathers excelled as fighters against the Turks and took part in the uprisings of 1684 and 1715; the deeds of two of them, Christos and Moschos Valaoras, were sung in popular ballads. But the Turks finally chased Moschos out of Epirus, and he and his

32

family settled on the island of Lefkas, where in recognition for his services the Venetian government granted him estates. Though reduced in number by the plagues that ravaged the country in the middle of the eighteenth century, the family managed to survive, and within three generations it had acquired both social position and wealth. One of its youngest members, John Valaoritis—as the family surname now appears—attached himself to the British naval forces in the Mediterranean, and, after a life of wide travel and shrewd commercial ventures, he returned to Lefkas, where he pursued a career of politics to become a distinguished deputy and senator in the Ionian Assembly.

Aristotelis Valaoritis, son of John, was born on September 1, 1824, into a family rich in tradition and steeped in national pride. The War of Independence was then still at its peak, and great events, such as the death of Byron, the fall of Missolonghi, and the naval battle at Navarino, were taking place in quick succession. Solomos had just composed his "Hymn to Liberty." Aristotelis grew up while the new Greece was being born and the atmosphere resounded with songs about the nation's fighters. Legends of brave chieftains—such as Katsandonis and Lambros Tjavellas, who had defended the region of Suli against the hordes of Ali Pasha—filled his imagination and helped shape his love for patriotic themes.

Meanwhile, his education was carefully designed to strike a happy medium between classical learning and knowledge of the history of the newborn Greek nation. His rich father provided private tutors—men like John Oikonomidis, a noted scholar and interpreter of Locric epigraphy, and Constantine Aisopios of the Ionian Academy at Corfu, where Aristotelis boarded for three years. He finished at the age of seventeen, and, accompanied by Oikonomidis, toured Greece to gain knowledge of his country. The two stopped at Athens, where the sensitive young man viewed the ancient ruins with Byronic gloom, lamenting the wretchedness of the present and contrasting it to Greece's glorious past. In 1842 he went to Italy, where within two years he obtained a *baccalaureat es lettres es sciences*. From there he travelled to Paris, where he studied law until 1846. He continued his studies in Pisa, Italy, and in 1847 was granted

a doctorate in law. As a student he was diligent and very
scholarly, though subject to fits of impulsive behavior. He was
especially proud of his knowledge of classical Greek, which
he used to impress his classmates and foreign tutors. The
following story, described in a letter to his mother, is typical
of this attitude:

While I was studying at Geneva, one of the professors of classical
Greek, who certainly knew much less classical Greek than I did,
wished to challenge me with one of the Pindaric odes, which I had
taken apart two years earlier with Oikonomidis. Well, I proved
the professor an ass, in fact, in front of his very colleagues. The
poor chap could not refuse me *la boule blanche*, to which he was
first to add *cum plauso*.[3]

Though he tackled law with earnest labor, it was evident that
his heart was not in this field. Often, while staying in Paris,
he would break away from his studies and pursue other kinds
of knowledge, particularly history and philosophy. Once, he
isolated himself in the country for six months and studied
German transcendentalism, the prevailing French mania of the
time. His love of nature, on the other hand, led him to daring
excursions, which included spectacular walking tours through
Switzerland, the Tyrol, and Italy. After the completion of his
doctoral studies, he visited France and England, and walked
through Scotland. These adventures nurtured his romantic nature
and fed his mind with ideas soon to be expressed in his early
poetry. Young Valaoritis must have passed through a period
of storm and stress (*Sturm und Drang*), for at times he was
seized by fits of remorse and a tendency toward nihilism that
was to survive through his life. One of his early poems, "Verse
B," of his first collection *Stichourgimata*, begins:

> Current of my youth, muddied by passions,
> Why do you flow toward the depths of nothing?
> Why doesn't the wind's raging blast
> Carry me where the deep sleep dwells?

Aristotelis was a youth of great physical robustness and
personal attractiveness. A typical romantic hero, he followed

the Byronic example of wandering through Europe, "living and loving." He was an expert swordsman and marksman, liked hunting and leisure, and enjoyed being handsome, rich, strong, and full of zest, "drinking life to the lees." In 1847 he visited the Tyrol, where he read the writings of Wallenstein and Schiller. In Venice he participated in some sort of uprising and was arrested by the Austrian police. At Naples he became so enraged with a spy who had trailed him day and night that he beat him up mercilessly, and then escaped the Bourbon police by boarding a British man-of-war that was moored in the harbor. Reckless abandon almost cost him his life once when, in Paris, he walked the streets alone at night and was attacked by two apaches; he killed one with a small stiletto that he always carried, and left the other for dead with a ferocious fist blow. But he himself received a near fatal wound in the ribs and had to fight for his life for forty days. In 1848, he took part in uprisings in Italy and Hungary, and in Budapest he was imprisoned during a popular uprising. A friend of his father's managed to rescue him from the Austrian police and sent him back home.

During those adventurous years he found time to compose a large number of poems, all in archaic idiom. Most of these poems remained unpublished and entirely unknown until many years after the poet's death.[4] But a slender volume appeared in 1847, titled *Stichourgimata* (*Verses*), containing four poems, all written in a mixed form of popular and archaic language. He must not have been very proud of them, because he rarely talked of his early poetry and, in 1868, omitted all four poems from the only complete edition of his work published during his lifetime. But the publication of *Stichourgimata* did not go unnoticed. A major critic,[5] writing in an influential newspaper, *Nea Hellas*, on August 1 of the same year, observed that Greece did not lack poetic talent, and he urged the young poet to create new national symbols by dramatizing Greece's struggle for liberty. *Stichourgimata* became a popular collection, and many throughout Greece memorized its contents.

While in Venice, Aristotelis met Eloisia Typaldos, daughter of Aimilios Typaldos, a Greek nobleman residing in Italy, and the liaison between the young lovers progressed rapidly.

She played patriotic songs on the piano for him, and he recited his verses. Typaldos, who had been active in a campaign to preserve Greek culture abroad, was favorably impressed by the young poet, and when Aristotelis visited Venice again with his father in 1851, the engagement took place, followed by the wedding a year later. The marriage was a happy one. Eloisia understood Valaoritis' character completely, and always supported him in his emerging political ambitions and literary aims. She became his lifelong mentor and confidante in literary and political matters, counselling and comforting her husband in moments of crisis. During his extended and frequent absences to the Ionian Assembly, and later to Athens, the poet wrote her long letters, describing in great detail a major part of his activities as a statesman and man of letters. Prudent and persevering, Eloisia remained in the background, patiently raising a family, while her husband, consumed by his burning energies, embarked on one of the most meteoric careers in modern Greece.

II *The Fight for the Union of the Heptanese with Greece*

Valaoritis continued his travels abroad until 1853, when he returned and settled at Lefkas with his wife. He was now twenty-nine, and he had gained considerable knowledge of the world; but he had yet to produce major poetry, although his studies of literature and interest in letters had intensified. His interest in politics had also increased sharply. His one great ambition, and the one that motivated his actions for some time, was to see the Heptanese—the seven Ionian islands—and the rest of "unredeemed" Greece liberated. No sooner did he arrive in Lefkas than he became involved in the movement then dominating Heptanesiac politics calling for the union of the Ionian islands under the British Protectorate with Greece.

In March 1857 he was almost unanimously elected deputy from Lefkas to the Ionian Assembly, and moved to Corfu to assume his new duties. During the same year he published his first major collection of poetry, *Mnemosyna (Memorial Songs)*, consisting of twelve poems, most of which extolled the feats of famous heroes during Greece's prerevolutionary period. This publication brought him immediate fame and considerably advanced his literary career. The Ionian critics, usually cautious in granting recognition, were impressed. As this event coincided with the death of Solomos, which occurred on February 16, 1857, Valaoritis was greeted as the new national poet of Greece. King Othon sent a representative to award Valaoritis the Cross of the Savior, an honor which the poet cherished all his life. Spiridon Trikoupis, a distinguished man of letters, compared Valaoritis to Solomos in a memorable short verse:

> The nightingale has not died
> The nightingale always lives;
> It changed its plumage,
> It did not change its voice.

Valaoritis' poetry also received notices in the foreign press. The Rumanian critic, Dora d' Istria,[6] wrote an article about *Mnemosyna*, accompanied by selected translations, that was printed in the French journal *Revue des Deux Mondes.* Valaoritis was also included in the bibliographical section of *Libre Recherche*. The Italian poet, Nicholas Tommaseo, wrote three long reviews of Valaoritis' poetry, published in *Diritto* of Turin.

For the next several years, Valaoritis maneuvered his way dexterously through the complicated politics of the Ionian Assembly, balancing his position between the Liberal party, which demanded immediate union, and the Reformists, who favored the continued British protection of the islands. Firm of character and decisive in his actions, the young poet won a reputation for his ardent patriotism and the torrential style of his speeches. Though a moderate where internal politics were concerned, he was unbending in his opposition to British protection and held steadily to a single objective—the speedy liberation of the seven islands. To that end, he would sacrifice "position and personal interest," he said in one of his early speeches, and was ready to give his "last penny," his children, his property, "everything," if needed.

These and his other activities alarmed the British, who tried by various means, including promises of high position, to win

Valaoritis to their side. Gladstone, who became high commissioner in 1859, made special efforts to befriend the poet,
obviously admiring both his literary achievements and his
political eminence. Valaoritis, who had by this time become
immensely popular and was recognized and cheered in the
streets of Corfu, declined all honors promised by the British,
adhering steadily to the purpose of union. When Gladstone pro-
posed a revision of the Ionian constitution, in accordance with
the progressive ideas of the nineteenth century, the Ionian
Assembly voted union with Greece, rejecting any other solution.
Valaoritis was chosen to draft the assembly's response in a
letter to Queen Victoria requesting the complete freedom of
the Ionian islands. With his usual zest, Valaoritis stayed up
an entire night, endeavoring to do his best. When he read his
draft before the assembly the following day, all members present
burst into frenzied applause. The letter was so well written
that even Gladstone was impressed, sending a note to Valaoritis
with his compliments. However, the draft was rejected by the
British government, and Gladstone made new proposals for the
improvement of the islands under the status quo.

In 1859, Valaoritis published a long historical poem, *Kyra
Phrosyni,* which was generally well received and added to his
literary reputation. King Othon once more expressed his satisfaction in a special message, and the poem was given favorable
notice both at home and abroad. After this publication, however, Valaoritis became totally immersed in political activities,
and his literary output between 1859 and 1864, the year of the
union, was slight. His political actions, however, were not con-
fined to the affairs of the Heptanese, since he also became
attached to other revolutionary causes around him. He took
part in an activist organization in Italy headed by Garibaldi
that had a broad network of local committees spread throughout the Balkans, aiming at the liberation of all nations under
the Turkish yoke and promoting the unification of Italy. Valaoritis generously contributed money and labor and often travelled
to Epirus and Montenegro as a representative of the Ionian
committee. The Italian uprising of 1860 had an impact on the
Ionian Assembly, and Valaoritis saw in it a parallel to Greek
aspirations. In supporting the uprising, he believed that what

he did for the freedom of others outside Greece should be
imitated by the Ionians. Consistent with this ideal, he issued
a proclamation at Lefkas on July 5, 1860, asking the Ionian
people to contribute to the Italian revolt.

Meanwhile, his position within the Ionian Assembly had
improved markedly. Suspected at first of conservatism, Valaoritis
managed to demonstrate that he was on the side of the unionists.
Padovas and Lombardos, two leading representatives from the
islands of Cephalonia and Zakynthos, were after a time convinced that the poet would not revert to the pro-British policies
of his family tradition. The English Protectorate tried to remove
him from power by rigging the elections of 1862 but failed, and
Valaoritis was elected by a large majority. The twelfth Ionian
Assembly spoke out even more strongly than the previous one
on the question of union. Hard pressed to defend his government's policies, the new high commissioner, Henry Storks, issued
a proclamation urging the deputies to abandon their struggle
for union and to concentrate instead on improving living conditions in the islands. Valaoritis, who drafted the assembly's
reply, easily overthrew the British argument by pointing out
that the islands' wretched conditions were mainly caused by
the heavy taxes exacted by the British government. Other in-
justices were mentioned: laws were not effectively enforced,
schools had deteriorated, freedom of speech was perilously
curbed, public administration was poor, even the constitutional
rights of the assembly were curtailed. The voice of the Ionian
people once more called for justice, and the only solution
possible was union. Valaoritis was present when a committee
handed the document to Storks, and later delivered a fiery
speech in the assembly which added to his popularity with
the unionists and the radicals.

The political situation in the Ionian islands changed abruptly
in 1862 with the overthrow of King Othon, and the ascension
of George, prince of Denmark, to the throne of Greece. Britain
announced that the seven islands would be given to Greece
as a gift from Queen Victoria to the Greek people. The event
was celebrated at Corfu on March 25, 1863, the Day of National
Independence, and Valaoritis, having composed for the occasion
a new poem, "The Rock and the Wave," recited it before a

crowd delirious with enthusiasm. On July 25, a referendum
was held to confirm the wishes of the people of the Heptanese
to unite with Greece.

Following these events, Valaoritis was elected first deputy
of Lefkas and again travelled to Corfu, where Commissioner
Storks asked the Ionian Assembly to vote on the queen's proposal. As usual, it was Valaoritis who drafted the reply. Some
of his colleagues were critical of a paragraph expressing gratitude
to the queen, but the document was corrected and read to
the chamber the following day in a scene of frenzied applause.
Valaoritis, though cheered wildly while reading the reply, was
denounced for proposing the acceptance of a British provision
that specified that King George I of Greece temporarily assume
all privileges hitherto exercised by the queen until a new
constitution was drawn. Valaoritis saw that this measure was
necessary for the preservation of law and order during the
difficult period of transition. His passion for liberty did not
obscure his political vision in this and other practical matters.
As his son writes:

Where national affairs were concerned, the judgment of Valaoritis
never allowed poetic imagination to interfere with the matter at
hand; one might say that he had the cool mind of a diplomat and
a prophetic ability to see through things. What he said and wrote
furnish ample evidence of this. He was able to perceive that two
sections of the same nation, having different law systems, and
different political and social organisms, cannot be unified without
certain precautionary and transitional measures or without certain
agreements reached in advance. . . . The situation in Greece, pre-
cariously close to civil war, demanded such measures.[7]

Valaoritis readily perceived that the Ionian Commonwealth
was a significant cultural and political center with a parliament
and an academy of letters. It would, therefore, be beneficial
if Corfu remained for a while the second capital of Greece in a
social, if not in a political sense. But his counsel was dis-
regarded. The quick change of government brought about the
confiscation of many estates of the nobles and, with it, the
resentment of the established social class of the Heptanese.
Law and order soon broke down. The Ionian gendarmery,

known for its discipline and devotion to duty, was disbanded. The Ionian Academy, the only institution in Greece that matched western institutions, was abolished. In fact, Corfu entered a period of slow decline and for a long time remained but a land of natural beauty and enchantment neglected by all except tourists and an occasional man of letters.

The Ionian Assembly was dissolved in May, 1864, and Valaoritis, with two other ex-deputies, departed for Athens to arrange the Ionian representation in the Greek National Assembly. In Piraeus and Athens big crowds cheered the Ionian representatives, calling them "brothers." Valaoritis and the two other Ionians were greeted by the members of the assembly and a host of dignitaries, among whom were Prime Minister Kanaris and young King George himself. The monarch was immediately attracted by the poet's candor, independence, and cosmopolitan attitude. Valaoritis, in turn, was impressed by the intelligence, kindness, and optimism of the youthful king. The meeting resulted in a bond of strong affection that lasted for a lifetime and harmonized perfectly with their political vision. Valaoritis saw that the country needed a steady hand to control party conflicts and to hold it on course for the national goals which included expansion of the borders and strengthening Greece's position in the East. This was the reason behind the promonarchy stance which he adopted immediately after the union and which cost him political sympathy among his former partners.

III   *Politics in Athens—Triumph and Defeat*

Valaoritis was elected first deputy of Lefkas to the Greek National Assembly in June 1864, and went to Athens one month later with the rest of the Heptanesiac deputies. There was another enthusiastic reception by the crowds, but Valaoritis realized at once that the political situation in Greece was critical. The Kanaris government rested on a thin majority, and the opposition of Voulgaris, Delegeorgis, and Grivas threatened to overthrow it. The Ionian deputies were ready to join the government, but the opposition tried to prevent them by rousing crowds to street demonstrations. Rumors circulated of impending uprisings and riots, and Valaoritis used his influence to calm boiling passions as best as he could. When the confirmation of the Ionian deputies took place a month later, Valaoritis was asked to speak to the assembly. When he spoke the chamber was filled to capacity with Athenian society, high-ranking officials, members of the church and government. The crowds outside were so large that they occupied the entire Constitution Square. Valaoritis was an inspiring orator and knew how to strike responsive chords in the hearts of fellow Greeks. Stringing patriotic images together with dexterous verbal artistry, he literally brought his audience to the brink of emotional frenzy. But in spite of its emotional appeal, the speech was conciliatory in tone and raised some important practical considerations. Valaoritis recommended avoidance of internal strife, continuation of the struggle to free the still unredeemed Greek lands, and a concerted effort to rebuild the countryside. Above all, he called for party conflict to cease and for all to remain faithful to the king and to the idea of national unity.

After this event, Valaoritis' popularity rose to its highest point, but he modestly avoided honors and declined the chairmanship of the national assembly offered him by the Kanaris government. The enthusiasm generated by his speech quickly evaporated, and the opposition once more staged street demonstrations in an attempt to embarrass and finally overthrow Kanaris. Valaoritis, remaining calm and faithful to his ideal of national unity, refused to ally himself with either party. He was developing a strong distaste for Greek national politics, but was still hopeful at this point·that he could play the role of mediator by providing conciliatory counsel to the rival factions and valuable advice to the young king who had taken a warmhearted interest in the poet and admired his forthrightness and character.

The assembly ended its sessions in November 1864, but Valaoritis remained in Athens for a while longer, exerting his influence to help Lefkas secure a prefecture. The island by now was considered part of the mainland rather than one of the seven Ionian islands, and had been administratively attached to the prefecture of Preveza. He also worked for the establishment of a bank of agriculture for the Heptanese, but his proposal was turned down for lack of funds. Despondent, he returned to Lefkas, pessimistic about the political future of Greece and disgusted with the politicians of Athens. When toward the end of the same year the ministry of foreign affairs was vacated, the position was offered to Valaoritis, and both king and government exerted great pressure on him to accept. He declined, faithful to the pledge he had given the Ionian deputies that he would not take a government post at this time. Besides, he was anxious to be with his family in the quiet atmosphere of his Lefkas home. A villa had just been built at Madouri, an islet near the Gulf of Vlychos which he had inherited from an elder cousin. Since early youth, Valaoritis loved to visit the island and there hunt and relax, away from the clamor and turbulence of the world. He settled comfortably and began the composition of *Athanasis Diakos*, a major poem that required extensive historical research.

He worked incessantly for several months, refusing to have anything to do with politics, even of the local sort. Nevertheless, interrupt he did, since he felt obliged to return to Athens in order to safeguard the interests of Lefkas, which was about to be deprived of its court and high school (*gymnasium*). The government of Alexandros Koumoundouros, then in power, offered Valaoritis a post, but he declined. Critical of this government's conduct in the last elections, Valaoritis attacked it in the assembly with a fervor that caused it to fall overnight. The next government also offered Valaoritis a post, but once more the irrepressible deputy from Lefkas refused to accept. Four governments followed one another in rapid succession, while Valaoritis, back at Madouri, held stubbornly to his independent position. He did go back to Athens, however, in an attempt to save the prefecture of Lefkas, which had in the meantime been established through his efforts. A post was offered him again, and this time he battled hard with his conscience before turning it down. Both the prefecture and court of Lefkas were duly abolished with his decline of the offer, and Valaoritis was back in Athens in January 1866, trying to secure a stay of this decision. But the assembly sessions were over by then, and his efforts proved futile. Embittered, he returned to Madouri and continued work on *Diakos*, finishing the poem in March of the same year. Another, shorter poem, "Astrapoyiannos," was composed in a moment of sudden inspiration while the poet was sitting at his marble desk outside his villa. The sudden death of his daughter Maria, named after an infant that had perished a few years earlier, interrupted these creative pursuits and plunged the poet into a period of mourning. But events of great moment soon arrived to distract him from his sorrow.

In December 1866, the Cretan Revolution broke out. Fearing the intervention of Turkey, the Greek government mobilized an army. Valaoritis was among the first to hasten to Athens to offer his services. He was tireless in his efforts, serving on the Cretan Committee and closely cooperating with the government of Koumoundouros, which was back in power. For a while, Valaoritis believed that the time of the liberation of the unredeemed Greek lands had arrived. He felt the excitement of anticipation. Against the advice of the French and English ambassadors, Corbineau and Erskine, he spoke in the national assembly on January 18, 1867, supporting government measures to increase the size of the army and prepare the nation for war. The speech, lasting an hour and a half, was one of his most spectacular, driving the crowds present to a delirium of applause. The government gained prestige by his speech, and Koumoundouros offered the poet the post of ambassador to the United States to enlist American sympathies in favor of the Greek cause in Crete. Once again, Valaoritis declined, considering his presence in Athens more important. The printing of *Diakos*, meanwhile, was progressing satisfactorily but needed supervision; a second edition of both the *Mnemosyna* and *Phrosyni* were also under way. These tasks kept Valaoritis busy, but not to the exclusion of politics. Utilizing the prestige he gained from his January oration, he succeeded in persuading the government, with another spectacular speech, to have the court of Lefkas reinstated. During the same year, he began writing a long epic poem, *The Poor Hormovitis*, a project meant to complete the cycle of epic poems relating the crimes of Ali Pasha against Greeks that he had begun with *Kyra Prosyni*.

The year 1867 stands out as the most successful in Valaoritis' political career; but it is also the year that marks his realization that he must eventually withdraw entirely from politics. When he returned to Athens in the fall, the Cretan question was extinct, and the political atmosphere generally oppressive. The office of deputy, so actively sought by the average Greek politician, had become disagreeable to Valaoritis. Though more than willing to further the general interests of his home island, he regretted having to do favors for anyone, and he felt humiliated when he was obliged to climb up and down the stairs of various ministries in order to take care of the petty chores and small personal obligations laid upon him by the electorate. "This is a slave's business," he used to say, alluding to the office of deputy.

He was also seriously concerned about the lawlessness prevailing in the countryside. The lack of state control, adequate courts, and a trained police force had reduced postwar Greece to chaos. Valaoritis deplored the shortage of schools and functioning courts. He complained frequently in his speeches that the people in the countryside had been abandoned to their own fate; the government had never shown the determination necessary to wipe out brigandage, construct roads, or help the development of agriculture. Valaoritis understood freedom as a means to provide enlightenment and discipline. He despised lawlessness and frequently blamed the government for failing to enforce measures necessary for an ordered and progressive society.

The elections of 1868 took place in an atmosphere of bitter discord, accompanied by heavy-handed government interference in many provinces and considerable wrangling by rival factions. Valaoritis was unwilling to run, but the pressure of his friends and his loyalty to Koumoundouros again prevailed. Although he emerged victorious, the methods of his opponents at Lefkas, who had attempted to prevent his friends from voting by using force, had a telling effect on his morale. Nevertheless, he hastened to Athens and joined a committee to investigate election irregularities. The party of Dimitrios Voulgaris had won almost every available seat, while Koumoundouros was soundly routed. Voulgaris was running the government dictatorially, and the members of the opposition were under police surveillance. Valaoritis was asked to join the government party, but he declined.

Dissatisfied with the slow progress of the committee, and generally dejected, he was about to retire to Lefkas for good when his famous quarrel with the Iakovatos brothers occurred and, like a *deux ex machina*, put an end to his political career. Since it throws light on the personality of Valaoritis, this incident deserves to be told in some detail.

The brothers George and Charalambos Iakovatos, deputies from the Ionian island of Cephalonia, were the ringleaders of the Voulgaris party and the most vocal members of a group attempting daily to intimidate the opposition. George Iakovatos, chairman of the committee investigating the elections, had recently published a libelous satiric volume against Heptanesiac poets, including Valaoritis. The antics of the Iakovatos brothers had aroused a great deal of criticism among Athenian society, and general indignation was at this moment mounting into a storm.

During one of the assembly sessions, on June 5, 1868, the opposition demanded the correction of the minutes of the previous day which had been so grossly distorted that even members of the government were outraged. As one deputy rose to protest, Charalambos Iakovatos also rose and called him a liar and a cheat. Zanos, a respected friend of Valaoritis, begged Iakovatos to restrain his words, because in insulting a deputy he insulted the assembly and the nation itself. Furious, Iakovatos turned on Zanos, calling him a cheat, a liar, and a thief. Unable to restrain himself any longer, Valaoritis approached Iakovatos and, "the blood boiling in his veins," told him that he would punish him if he did not stop offending his friends. Iakovatos began laughing derisively. "Then," Valaoritis says (in a letter describing the incident), "I gave him such a slap in the face that he toppled over. His brother rose from his seat and attacked me, but I delivered such blows that I wondered where my strength was coming from."[8]

Enraged, the government of Voulgaris asked for the dismissal of Valaoritis from the assembly and for penal action to be taken against him. But the assembly, fearing public opinion, decided only to censure the poet. Valaoritis never again participated in an assembly discussion. When his turn came for reelection, early in 1869, he strongly resisted the pressures from his friends at Lefkas and Athens and refused to run again.

The Iakovatos incident, which has become a point of controversy among some critics, explains the paradox of Valaoritis' brilliant but unfulfilled political career. Politics for him meant uncorrupted ethical standards, impeccable behavior, and dignity. The members of the Ionian Assembly possessed these qualities to a large extent, and when Valaoritis was transplanted into the Athenian political arena he could not stand the sight of the wrangling, petty figures who should have been advancing the interests of the young nation. The reality of Athens was ugly in contrast to the ideal world of the heroic figures woven into the myths of his poetry. As Emmanuel Roidis observes, the Iakovatos incident provided Valaoritis with a long-sought chance to return to his retreat, Madouri, where he lived "in a constant dream," amid the ghosts of the old klephts. Basically, Roidis feels, Valaoritis was a man divorced from reality, living not in the present, but in the past. "With today's people," Roidis says, "his muse never came into contact; only the blows of his fist did."[9]

For as long as he took an active part in politics, however, Valaoritis showed an astute judgment and an ability to handle practical matters. Another major commentator on his life and art, Kostis Palamas, observes that "Valaoritis did not merely serve in the Greek Assembly but he lived and acted like a genuine statesman."[10] Quoting supporting evidence from the works of Timoleon Philimon and Alexandros Vyzantios, Palamas makes the claim that the political life of Valaoritis equalled his poetic achievement. The deputy from Lefkas did, for instance, support such measures as the increase of imports to the Heptanese. He spoke out about tax reforms and land and sea transportation, helped reestablish the court at Lefkas, and was instrumental in resolving numerous issues on both the national and local levels. He was too conscientious and too compassionate to overlook even the slightest demand made upon him by his electorate. Yet even Palamas finally admits that Valaoritis was too idealistic and his poetic spirit too diverse to last the wear and tear of everyday politics.

Valaoritis spent the summer of 1869 at Lefkas, writing the

narrative poem, *Poor Hormovitis,* in which he describes the destruction of Hormovos, a village at Epirus, by Ali Pasha. The action of the poem reflects his agitation of soul; it depicts a parallel to the Turks' destruction of Crete, which followed the Greek government's cowardly withdrawal of its support. Crete was betrayed and, like Hormovos a century earlier, left to the wolves. *Poor Hormovitis* was finished and submitted to a publisher, Pavlos Lambros, in Athens. Valaoritis retrieved the manuscript for last minute corrections, but unfortunately he lost it with his luggage while stopping en route to Lefkas from Athens. The manuscript was never found and despite his many efforts the poet was unable to remember any part of it except a few of its beginning verses.

IV   *Retreat to Madouri—Last Years*

Withdrawal from politics was now final. Valaoritis could see no hope for an orderly succession of the Voulgaris government, which, in the meantime, had fallen. He thought that parliamentary life would be nothing more than a collision of parties trying to grab authority. Passions, quarrels, revenge would be the fruits of a political career. Meanwhile, the poet realized that he had neglected his personal affairs. For eighteen years he had had no surcease from politics. The fact that he had always been generous with contributions to causes and the expenses of election campaigns had an adverse effect on his finances. Now that his children were growing, the necessity of increasing his income became imperative. There was another source of worry. His heart was weakened by the disease that would eventually bring him to an early grave. From 1869 on, the pains in his chest became frequent, diminishing his vitality, though not his zeal for work or his devotion to his family duties. Fearing that his children might become impoverished after his death, Valaoritis threw his waning energies into the cultivation of his fields at Lefkas and at Madouri, where he had planted vines and olive groves. He loved farming—becoming a regular Greek Cincinnatus—and had a great deal of practical knowledge on agricultural matters.

Working in the fields gave him a chance to be in close contact with country people and to learn their ways and spoken language. Life at Madouri enabled him to be in touch with villagers and fishermen, and, no matter how busy or ill, he never stopped being inquisitive and curious. He travelled frequently across the channel to Acarnania, mostly on business or to hunt, and studied the language and customs of the people of Sterea Hellas. He was a keen observer and a methodical compiler of information and, despite his many interests, a fairly good linguist and folklorist. The material gathered in these researches found its way into his prefaces and the numerous commentaries and glossaries accompanying his poems. He was intent on documenting his belief that in the customs and habits of the people one could find indelible traces and undisputed proof of the genuineness of the Greek race. In this respect, living in the country afforded him the satisfaction that he was still working for his country's cause, and the farmer was not altogether divorced from the fighter for freedom nor the man of letters from the literary historian.

Though far from the national political scene, Valaoritis continued to exert some influence on local politics. His own immense fame and the high social position of his family made it difficult for him to avoid the role of leadership expected of him in the always factious politics of Lefkas. He was frequently petitioned by the former friends made during his early campaigns to intervene on their behalf with the government to solve one petty problem or another. This worried and distracted him, since politicizing of any kind always meant some anguish for him. Such involvement in local affairs—and he was conscientious enough to always comply with requests—deprived him of valuable time that could have been devoted to his writing. For these and other reasons, his literary production during his later years was minimal. In 1869, a strong earthquake shook Lefkas, killing some of his best friends and almost trapping his own family under the debris. The year 1870 was full of family cares and problems of practical nature, and passed with no literary output. In 1871, he wrote only one poem, "Kyra Phaneromeni," an ode to the Virgin, local protectress of the island.

Later in the same year, he received an invitation from the

rector of the University of Athens to recite a poem at the
ceremonies honoring the unveiling of the statue of Patriarch
Gregorios V, on March 25, the Day of Greek Independence.
Valaoritis felt hesitant at first, fearing that the effort might be
a strain on his weak heart. He finally accepted, asking only to be
permitted to compose and recite the poem in the demotic, the
language of the people. When this was granted him, he isolated
himself at Madouri, and laboriously composed a poem that
was to become a lasting memorial in the modern Greek popular
imagination. Though his work was interrupted several times
by various events, including an invitation from the king to
reenter politics (which he again rejected), he remained at
Madouri through the winter of 1872, occupied with such problems as the poem's language, content, and structure. He was
so absorbed in his work that he forgot about politics in Athens,
and for a time his spirits rose considerably.

The recitation of the poem on March 25, before a large crowd
under the blue Attic sky, "barely shaded by a few clouds,"
was a triumph, perhaps the poet's greatest. The "Ode to Patriarch
Gregorios V," though not one of his best poems, had nevertheless
those ingredients especially appealing to a fiercely nationalistic
crowd. His popularity reached new heights after this event. The
newspapers wrote eulogies; the foreign embassies, the literati
of Athens, and even the European press took note. Greeks
everywhere, at home and abroad, sent their congratulations.
Thousands of people visited him to offer compliments. But
the intensely emotional moment took its toll; as he returned to
his hotel, his pulse rose to 150 beats per minute, and he felt
that had the recitation lasted one moment longer, he would
have collapsed in front of the crowd. His health deteriorated
steadily from this point on. But this was a time of excitement,
of revived hope for a unified Greece, and Valaoritis basked
in the sun of his glory for a brief moment. A triumphant reception awaited him at Lefkas a few days later, where the
poet was awarded a gold medal and was carried through the
streets by a delirious crowd.

But his triumph was soon followed by a shocking disappointment. As he was stopping at Corfu on his way to Venice to
visit his father-in-law in the spring of 1872, he noticed in a

local newspaper a savage attack by an anonymous critic on his poem "Gregorios." The author, who turned out to be the noted man of letters and dramatist Dimitrios Vernardakis, picked the poem apart with pedantic zeal, at the same time challenging Valaoritis' unofficial designation as the national poet of Greece. Valaoritis immediately wrote a point by point refutation of this article and published it in the same newspaper, but he could not restrain his anger and bitterness. His poetic reputation had not been faring well with the critics. *Diakos*, the poem he had worked harder than any other to complete, had had a cool reception among the Athenian critics. And the Heptanesiac critics and scholars—among whom were Panayotis Panas and Iakovos Polylas—jealous of his ascendancy at the expense of Solomos, never quite recognized him as one of their own school. At the same time, Valaoritis had not contributed to his own cause. After 1866, the date of the publication of *Diakos* and a new edition of his older poetry, his literary output had been negligible. A combination of ill health, family problems, and disillusionment with politics had produced a slow and steady erosion in his literary ambitions.

From August 1872 on, Valaoritis spent most of his remaining years at the islet of Madouri. His visit to Venice convinced him that he could not rely on his father-in-law's estates to insure his children's financial future. He, therefore, plunged with renewed zeal into the task of improving his income. The environment at Madouri enchanted and fascinated him. He would have been pleased to stay there indefinitely, but unfortunately, his heart condition continued to worsen, and he frequently had to return to town where he was under a doctor's care. In spite of his laborious efforts, the expected financial recovery did not materialize, and he continued to be burdened with financial problems which further inhibited his literary activity. Inspiration returned to him occasionally, but he lacked stamina and was forced to abandon many projects when barely begun. One of these, *Gogos*, the story of a traitor who helped the infamous Ali Pasha destroy Parga, went only as far as an introductory chapter, which was published in the *Attic Calendar* in 1874.

Another care of these last years was the education of his two growing sons, Ioannis and Amilios. Ioannis, the elder son,

finished the gymnasium at Lefkas and entered the law school
of the University of Athens; the younger, Aimilios, brilliant
and impulsive, became a subject of much concern to his parents.
He finished the Lefkas gymnasium in 1873 and after much
family deliberation was sent to Leipzig, Germany, where he
intended to study "practical matters." Instead, he turned to
the study of poetry and the German poets with such a passion
that he forgot his initial goal. Valaoritis objected to this turn
of events, but was able to sympathize with his son's inclinations.
Father and son were temperamentally in perfect accord and
corresponded frequently. Aristotelis provided counsel on the
study of literature, while Aimilios showed talent for criticism
and offered some keen remarks on his father's poetry. This
lively correspondence brightened the somewhat gloomy years,
1873 and 1874, which the poet spent mostly in isolation and
poor health, while his wife was ever in Venice tending to her
sick and aging father. The deaths of many friends and relatives
during that period added to his melancholy mood; at times he
suffered from nightmares and even had visions and hallucinations.

In 1875, he nearly had another bout with politics. The party
of Charilaos Trikoupis, which had come to power at that time,
sought to curb the prestige of the Valaoritis family by supporting
a candidate from a rival family in Lefkas, Georgios Servos, who
ran against Aristotelis' brother, Xenophon. Remembering the
days of old, Valaoritis emerged from his isolation and cam-
paigned for his brother so fiercely that Xenophon won easily
over Servos. On the election day Valaoritis improvised a speech
to the people of Lefkas in which he attacked the Trikoupis
government a bit too imprudently, hinting at a popular uprising.
He was promptly accused of treason in the Athenian press.
For a fortnight he had to work hard, writing letters and
memoranda to friends in the government protesting his innocence. The election was annulled, nevertheless. When it was
repeated, the poet refused to have anything to do with it, staying
locked in his house that day. Yet Xenophon was elected again,
with a majority greater than before.

Another disaster struck in October 1875. Valaoritis' daughter
Nathalia died in Venice, where she was staying with her mother.
This blow was hard to bear, and Valaoritis plunged once more

into one of his dark moods. His deep sorrow is reflected in a short elegy, generally acknowledged as one of his finest lyrics. In January 1876 he went to Athens, feeling the need to see many of his old friends and to help his brother Xenophon establish himself as a deputy. He was given a warm reception by his former friends and acquaintances and was acclaimed "the poet of the Patriarch" by the crowds in the streets. He wrote a few poems, but found that any effort tired him easily, and he could not participate in social events with his former zest. "I have grown old," he wrote Aimilios, "and my poor health does not allow me excursions to Mt. Helicon."[11] A committee of young poets asked him to recite one of his poems on the occasion of the Greek Independence Day, but he declined, fearing a heart attack. He also declined another offer by Koumoundouros to accept the post of minister of foreign affairs. But new developments in the international arena kept him in Athens, in spite of his poor health. There were signs of an impending collision between Russia and Turkey, and Greece hoped to gain territory in Thessaly, Crete, and Epirus as a result of the scuffle. The Bulgarians were also claiming territory within the Thracian borders, and their relations with the Turks remained tense. There was excitement in the air, and Valaoritis smelled gunpowder like a war horse. Suddenly depression and considerations about his health were forgotten, and he wanted to live and see the outcome. He became a member of the Central National Committee, empowered to deal with foreign diplomatic matters. He seemed revived.

In the summer of 1877, during a visit to his father-in-law in Venice, his health again took a turn for the worse, and he felt his strength departing while the great event that he had waited for all his life, the war against Turkey and the final solution of Greek territorial claims, was drawing near. He felt the suspense of the approaching national drama but was at the same time aware that he would be unable to play a role in it. Valaoritis was now seriously ill. During the winter of 1877, he suffered from acute respiratory problems, while his heart condition grew steadily worse. And yet, he never stopped working, tending to his estates and caring for their improvement. He was ever ready to leap into local political activity, writing memoranda and endorsing friends for various positions at Lefkas. His correspondence with Aimilios shows important insights into poetry, its methods and techniques, prosody, and literary criticism. His spirit was alert, fervent, and enthusiastic, despite his physical decline.

He found time to write some poetry, and he composed "Kanaris" and "Eustathios Kondaris," both on the occasion of the death of friends. A great number of his shorter poems of this period were, in fact, funeral elegies. Death preoccupied and fascinated him, and writing about it was perhaps a means of soothing his own fears of an early expectation of it. Toward the end of 1877, he corresponded extensively with Emmanuel Roidis for several months, exchanging views on various literary matters, especially on the question of language. Valaoritis felt flattered that a man of the literary repute of Roidis would assign to him such a high place among Greek poets. In his first letter, Valaoritis wrote a long diatribe on the demotic, trying to impress the slightly condescending and somewhat cynical Roidis, who at any rate listened sympathetically to his Heptanesiac friend. This correspondence acted like a balm on Valaoritis' troubled last years, especially after the attacks of Vernardakis. It enabled him to remain in touch with the main literary events at the capital and to express an opinion on poets and poetry.

He now regretted that his ardent political activities of the past had deprived him of valuable time that could have been devoted to literature. The loss of the long poem, *The Poor Hormovites*, had robbed him of additional literary fame. In fact, Valaoritis was better known among the common people for his fervent patriotism and political activities than for his literary achievements. Had he lived longer, he might have achieved a greater literary reputation, especially if his last poem, *Photeinos*, had been completed and published during his lifetime. The letters to Roidis show good knowledge of the basic precepts of literary criticism and also an ability for objective analysis of his own works.

The Russo-Turkish War broke out in the meantime, and Valaoritis noted with disappointment the Greek government's passivity and lack of commitment in supporting the claims of the peoples of Epirus and Thessaly, who might have used this as an opportunity to gain their freedom. When he was a member of the Central National Committee, he had stated that Greek governments should never again encourage unredeemed Greeks to an uprising unless they intended to give active support or to intervene. He recalled how the Greek government had backed off from aiding Crete during the Cretan Revolution of 1866, and he was full of apprehensions that in a similar situation Greece would display again its lack of decisiveness. Even in his weakened condition he worked hard, sending letters and memoranda to his friend Koumoundouros and other men in Athens, urging them to take action. The Treaty of San Stefano, on March 3, 1878, between Russia and Turkey, creating a "Big Bulgaria,"[12] came as shocking news; he saw the interests of Greece ignored totally by the European powers, and the cause of Epirus lost, at least for the immediate future. Once more, his dream of a Greece liberated in its entirety was shattered. Yet, he found strength to send trusted guides from Lefkas who helped secure the passage of Greek volunteer soldiers across the border and into free Greece.

In the summer of 1878, Valaoritis travelled to Murano, Italy, to arrange for the transportation to Athens of the large library of his father-in-law, Typaldos, who had died earlier in the year. He spent some time there sorting out and packaging the books, which Typaldos had donated to the Greek National Assembly. His health improved somewhat with this rather pleasant occupation, and when he returned to Lefkas in the fall he was in better spirits. But more bad news was around the corner. His son Aimilios, who had again changed his field of study and had excelled in microbiology, working on his doctorate at the University of Iena, suddenly fell ill. His health broke down completely and he was near death. When Valaoritis heard the news, Aimilios had already left for Madeira with his mother in search of a better climate. Concern for his son added, of course, to Valaoritis' cares, and he now feared that he would die without having all the members of his family around him. But he continued to correspond with friends and relatives both at home and abroad, easing his pain somewhat.

Meanwhile, Greece and Turkey had engaged in negotiations

concerning the arrangements of the borders brought about by
the agreement at Berlin in July 1878, superceding the Treaty
of San Stefano. A provision allowed that Greece would acquire
territory in Thessaly and Epirus, and a Greek-Turkish committee
was formed to work out the details. Ships had arrived outside
the port of Preveza, and Valaoritis watched from his window,
growing impatient with both the proceedings and the Turks,
who procrastinated in their usual fashion. He knew that he had
little time to live, and he wanted the business of the borders
settled. He took the opportunity to feast the Greek members
of the committee at his house at Lefkas; for a moment he felt
revived. As news from Madeira was momentarily good, inspiration returned to him, and he translated the 33rd Canto of Dante's
Inferno in two days, in January 1879. The following month, he
started writing *Photeinos*, a heroic poem with subject matter
taken from the history of Lefkas, the place of his birth. He
finished the first canto of three hundred verses, but the effort
exhausted him, and he had to rest for two weeks. The spring
of 1879 was a quieter period, as news from Madeira continued
to be favorable. The committee at Preveza had come to nothing,
and the ships had departed. Valaoritis spent much of his time
sitting in front of his window gazing with longing at the
mountains of Epirus, the land of his ancestors, which he was
destined never to see liberated.

As his health improved slightly, Ioannis, who had stayed near
his father all this time and was exhausted himself, left for
Italy to recuperate. But in July bad news arrived from Madeira
again; Aimilios had suffered a relapse and was near death.
Valaoritis continued to write anxious letters, encouraging his
son and his wife as best as he could. But his own stamina
gave way, and he abandoned the writing of *Photeinos*, which
in the meantime had progressed to its third canto. Anxiety
over the illness of Aimilios had had a cumulative effect on his
own condition. He had already lost three daughters and several
relatives; death had wrought havoc with his family—too many
had perished. Philosophy and religion could no longer comfort
him. Yet, he did not resent his own approaching end; he had
lived his life and had reaped honors and rewards in abundance.
But why should the young die? "Nature is unrelenting, cruel,"

he was writing Aimilios. "She does not give a penny for our misfortunes, perhaps because she does not know that they are misfortunes but simply transformations of life, necessary phases for the existence of beings.... That is how it must be, but I seem unable to understand such truths."[13]

Better news arrived soon from Madeira, but too late. The poet had succumbed on July 24, at dawn. He was nearly fifty-five years of age. Knowing that his end was approaching, he confessed, took communion, gave his last instructions regarding family matters, and, uttering the names of his wife and children, he passed away. None of his family were with him. But he was lucky enough to die without seeing either the failure of Greece to acquire Epirus—or the successive deaths of three of his four remaining children, Aimilios, Andreas, and Olga.

Valaoritis' funeral was arranged by his fellow citizens, who mourned their beloved poet bitterly. His death was noted in Athens, as well as in the Italian and French press. An obituary written by Anastasios Byzantios in *Nea Imera* perhaps summarizes best public opinion about Valaoritis:

He lived and died from his heart. Perhaps others were more brilliant politicians, better orators, more expert in controlling their poetic inspirations; but no one compares with the former deputy from Lefkas and poet of the *Mnemosyna* in purity of political convictions and force and originality of poetic passion. In this prosaic century, when everyone remains attached to earthly interests, he alone lived constantly in another world, creating and becoming the priest of an ideal Greece.... Bringing together the noblest impulses of the heart, he made poetry a part of patriotism and patriotism a part of poetry.... He has left his mark both on the national history and in the history of letters.[14]

The poet was buried in the family mausoleum behind the church of Pantokrator at Lefkas. With his entire family absent, no decision could be made by friends whether his remains should be carried to Madouri, where he had passed some of his most serene hours.

CHAPTER 3

Early Poetry—From the Purist
to the Demotic

I Poems in the Patriarcheas Edition

THE first poems written by Valaoritis remained unpublished
and completely unknown until 1937, when an Athenian
scholar, Vasilios Patriarcheas, discovered them by accident.[1]
Though of meager literary value, these poems are worth examining for several reasons. Their sheer bulk alone is amazing—
approximately 3,500 lines—considering that this is about one-
third of the entire poetic production of Valaoritis. The poems
are written in a stiff archaic idiom ("super" *katharevousa*), an
idiom vehemently denounced by Valaoritis in his mature poetry.
This fact may explain why the poems were suppressed, although
Stichourgimata, a collection published in 1847, is also written
in this idiom. But the importance of these poems probably lies
elsewhere, for they show the influences of many authors of
antiquity and of modern times in a way that his later poetry
does not. While in his mature poetry references and allusions
to classical literature and history are methodically excluded, in
the original poems of this collection one finds evidence that
Valaoritis had taken an unusually strong interest in classical
antiquity early in his career—an interest that subsided in his
later years. One can easily trace influences from Homer, Theocritus, Pindar through the numerous allusions to classical history
and mythology. The influence of Dante is particularly strong;
there are also strong traces of Byronic influence and German
transcendental philosophy. Of the Greek authors, Valaoritis is
closer to Kalvos and Solomos in these early poems than at any
other point in his career. The influence of the Greek folk song, so
evident in his later poetry, and so important in the shaping of
his poetic method, is totally absent in these poems.

The poems in the Patriarcheas edition have several other noteworthy characteristics. Unlike the epic compositions of the later years, they are mostly lyrical, expressing the poet's own emotions and ideas. The German transcendental philosophy which he studied in his youth[2] is much more apparent in these poems than in any of his later works. Patriotism, an element always strong and pervasive in the poetry of Valaoritis, is evident, but it is expressed mostly in abstract terms. The poet dedicates whole passages to the praise of "goddess Freedom," or "goddess Glory" (he also uses other abstractions, such as "harmony," "beauty," "honor," frequently), but he never narrates concrete episodes from the Greek fight for freedom, as he does in his later poetry. Patriotism is to a large extent expressed as ancestor worship, but the ancestors mentioned are the ancient Greeks rather than his forefathers from the region of Epirus. There are also references to Greek historical events—the battles of Marathon and Salamis, for example—and to names and characters in Greek mythology.

The Patriarcheas poems can be divided into three general groups: first, there are nineteen original poems, all of which must have been written before Valaoritis had reached the age of twenty-three;[3] second, there are translations of ten (some are fragmentary) of the *Idylls* of Theocritus; third, there are miscellaneous fragments and different versions of poems already known and published during Valaoritis' lifetime. The existence of these last, along with the others found in 1937, led Patriarcheas to the conclusion that Valaoritis had all the early poems in his possession until 1875—a conjecture allowing him to believe that the poet had deliberately hidden their existence for reasons that remain unknown. Though the Theocritus translations are of some interest—showing Valaoritis a competent translator and an expert user of the purist, and also explaining the Theocritian elements in his poetry—it is the nineteen original poems that are worth some consideration.

Among these original compositions, "The Ocean" is one example of the purist language used effectively to convey a sense of grandeur. The ocean (becoming "the sea" in his subsequent poems) is a potent symbol, exhibiting a dualism that was to become a permanent mark in many poems of

Valaoritis. At times, the ocean is "calm, graceful, smiling, playing with the sand," but it can change aspect quickly, becoming
furious and raging in a storm. Somewhat like Shelley's wind
in "Ode to the West Wind," the ocean is personified, becoming
a spiritual entity and assuming meaning in allegorical terms.
The allegory here, however, is not as sharply drawn and relevant as in "The Rock and the Wave," or in other later poems.
Worth noting in "The Ocean" is an allusion to John Milton
(lines 24–30), "the blind singer whom old Albion refused to
praise and to honor," revealing that young Valaoritis had absorbed English literary influences during his studies.

Equally interesting are "Last Night in the Life of Marco
Botzaris," which describes in vivid terms a famous chieftain's
charge against the Turkish post at Karpenisi (1823) and his
heroic death; and "To my Friend Pangalos," in which the young
poet expresses his desire to see his motherland while away
in Switzerland: "Ah, when will I be able to kiss the bones of
my ancestors, no matter how rotten or worm-eaten they are!"
Many poems are formal compositions—the purist is particularly
suited for formal expression—with ponderous beginnings, and
invocations to the muse Polyhymnia. Of particular interest are
a series of love poems ("Erotics") in which the young poet
displays his "sensuous" side—a side totally suppressed in his
mature poetry. In "Desire," for instance, the poet finds himself
in a forest wooing the nymph Sikelia, to whom he declares passionate love. In another poem, the poet, standing near a river-
bank, is ravished by the appearance of a "naked youth," god
Eros himself who smites him with his arrow, wounding him
cruelly.

In "Song I" the poet addresses Phoebus, the god of light,
as he is about to descend in the west and "dip into the night."
Phoebus must tell the Creator that the young poet stands where
the bones of his ancestors are buried and is ashamed for being
a slave. "The bones of slaves cannot inhabit the same space
as those of free men," the poet mutters to himself mournfully.
In "Song II" the poet's mind is filled with transcendental images
of God and nature: "I see the divine splendor of being, but not
the Lord of beings." He urges Phoebus to rise and greet the
"shadows of his ancestors," before they disappear with the

coming day. Another poem, "Harmony," is a hymn inspired
by the beauty of Greek nature as the young poet remembers
it while away in Switzerland; he asks Hellas to listen to him,
"her son." He urges his fellow Greeks to climb the mountains
where they will be free, at the same time exhorting himself to
be worshipful of freedom. With characteristic Byronic gloom,
he walks alone among the mountains of Switzerland: "I walked
and dark clouds of melancholy shaded my spirit." Then again his
desire for freedom is expressed in taut phrases:

> Better lie, insensitive, under a grove's cypresses
> Than live enslaved, with sighs and sorrows,
> Under the shadow of a scepter.

Perhaps the most successful work in this collection is "Verses
Written on the Last Day Before my Departure for Switzerland,"
a poem consisting of fifty-six stanzas of an *aabbccdd* rhyme
scheme, and showing some complexity in both versification and
structure.[4] Here patriotism is blended dexterously with ancestor
worship and with feelings of despondence and loneliness as
the young man prepares to depart from his native land. Freedom, personified in the manner of Solomos, addresses the
enslaved Greeks of the Ionian islands, exhorting them to rise
and throw off the foreign yoke. Recalling the heroic acts of
his ancestors, the young poet warns England—the modern
Rome!—that goddess Freedom has always been on the side of
the oppressed, and that she will aid them in their efforts to
punish the oppressors. As he departs for Switzerland, he bids
farewell to his native land with sentimental phrases reminiscent
of the opening cantos of Byron's *Childe Harold*. The poem ends
with vows and promises to return—truly a liberator of his
country—and with more warnings to England should she insist
on keeping the islands under her yoke.

The importance of the Patriarcheas poems has been ably
summed up by the Greek critic Kleon Paraschos:

These poems add little that is very significant to his mature production—as indeed is the case with the later written *Stichourgimata*.
But in a way (a historical, that is, not an organic way) they com-

plete the picture of the personality of the poet. They show how
the young man moved in his first steps, what subjects attracted
him, how he handled his material, and what abilities he had in
dealing with compositions of some length. They show us something
even more important—that with poets, even with great poets, what
we call "personality" may take time to develop fully.[5]

II   Stichourgimata

Stichourgimata (1847), Valaoritis' first published poetry collection, consists of four poems: "The Klepht," "Poem II,"
"Lefkatas," and "The Convict." The first and last are dramatic
narratives, while the second and third are shorter lyrics. In
language and subject matter, these four poems do not differ
much from the previously discussed "unpublished poems," but
some improvement of the young poet's technique is noticeable,
while the purist has become less pompous and easier to understand. In fact, in the first poem, "The Klepht," the language
is much closer to the demotic than to the purist. With the
publication of *Stichourgimata,* Valaoritis became a known
poet, but the suppression of his early poetry and the omission
of *Stichourgimata* from the complete edition of his works in
1868 show that throughout his life he held the poetry of his
youth in low esteem.

Aside from the ease in handling language and the elements
of the demotic, the first poem, "The Klepht," has little to
recommend it. It relates the love affair of a fighter, Kitzos, with
a Greek girl who has been abducted by a ferocious Turkish
chief, Hassan. Kitzos descends from the mountains with his
companions, and fights and kills Hassan, who had in the meantime killed the girl. Kitzos carries her to the mountains, where
he commits suicide over her body.

"Poem II," second in the collection, is less diffuse than the
previous one and, though written in the archaic idiom, it is
quite readable and helps us understand the young poet's mind
and inclinations. It is written in fifteen syllable lines, which
the poet has now begun to handle with some authority. The
poem's opening verses are quite well known: "Current of my
youth, why are you running toward the depths of nothing?"

Assuming a Byronic pose, the poet contemplates the constant loss of his youth, as years are going by fast. He already sees himself in a tomb—but isn't the tomb preferable to the chains of tyrants? The tomb is a quiet place, away from the turbulence of society and the storms of nature, and is depicted as an "oasis in the sandy desert of his youth." But even in the tomb he will not be able to find perfect peace; not if he has forgotten his patriotism and his duty: "As long as my country's soil is still enslaved, I will remain alive to shout, revenge!"

In the third poem, "Lefkatas" (Cape Lefkatas), the poet uses an elaborate metaphor. The cape is a famous national monument, depicted by Virgil in the *Aeneid*, and known in popular myths as the place from which the poetess Sappho leaped into the sea after a disappointment in love. At the time the poet views it, the cape has aged, beaten by winds and storms over the centuries. Once Zeus had sat on its top dressed in eagle's wings; now only poor and hungry shepherds in rags roam about it. On its highest rock was once the temple of Apollo; now only leaves and brush exist in the desolate landscape. "Glory is mortal and dies," the poet exclaims as he views the scene. In older times, a sailor seeing the cape on the horizon would fall on his knees and offer prayers; "Now times have changed, the sailor is not afraid, scarcely noticing you as he goes by." No one walks there now; no one respects the sacred place. Where once priests sang holy songs, now birds are heard to croak. This mournful dirge, detailing the glories of the past and the wretchedness of the present (allegorically reflecting the past glories of Greece and its present plight), is interrupted by some hopeful lines which reveal the patriotism that one would guess was at the bottom of each thought and trope of the poem:

> Sleep, Lefkatas, sleep, perhaps an hour will come
> When your poor country will rise again;
> Instead of the croaks of wild birds
> You might hear songs—the voices of liberty!

The last poem, titled "The Convict," is a lengthy melodramatic monologue telling the story of Elias, a prisoner dying in his

dungeon. In this poem, Valaoritis creates an atmosphere of
horror—very similar to that found in his later poetry—with visions,
ghosts, and other details of the Gothic tradition. Sitting in
his cell, the prisoner is awakened in the middle of the night
by a rooster's crowing; then he sees visions, shadows that have
come to haunt and torment him. The candle is blown out by
a "fiery mouth"; there is thunder outside, the prison shakes;
deep darkness prevails in the dungeon, while ghosts "dance
about." The noises increase; sounds, horrible, confused, come
from the mouths of the dead: "Awake, Rise, Elias!" they cry.
The shadows continue to torment him until dawn comes. Then
they depart. A few days later, a frozen body is hanging by a
piece of wood outside in the prison yard, its arms swaying in
the wind, as if the dead man were counting time.

In its vivid creation of a fantastic and nightmarish atmosphere, the poem seems more to follow the tradition of Edgar
Allan Poe than that of Dante. Though the language remains stiff
and pompous, the details are given with eloquent vividness and
the imagery is more concrete here than in any previous poem.
Interestingly enough, this is the only poem of the four in the
collection where the patriotic theme is almost entirely missing.

III   Mnemosyna

Ten years intervened between the publication of *Stichourgimata* and that of *Mnemosyna* (*Memorial Songs*), another
poetry collection, in 1857. During this time, Valaoritis had
returned from his wanderings abroad, had settled down at
Lefkas and married, and had embarked on a busy and active
political career. Meanwhile, his views on language had changed
radically, his technique had matured, and the scope of his
poetry narrowed considerably with the elimination of nearly
all themes not related to Greece's struggle for liberation. The
language is perhaps the most remarkable change, because the
composition of *Mnemosyna* was meant to be an emphatic
rejection of *katharevousa* in favor of the demotic, the popular
idiom, which the poet had taken great pains to study and in
which he would write all his poetry from this point on.

In a letter to his father-in-law, Aimilios Typaldos, which

served as a preface to the collection, Valaoritis stated his basic beliefs regarding the role of the demotic in modern Greek poetry. "The language of the people," he said, "must also become the language of Greek poetry."[6] Greek poets, Valaoritis insisted, have an unusual advantage over poets of other nations in that they have "an entire dialect, the demotic, for their exclusive use. No other language is composed entirely of popular idioms. On the other hand, the purist has been nothing but a burden to Greek poets, a yoke heavier than that of the Turks to bear."[7] It must therefore be abandoned; Greeks must free themselves from it, and it is the duty of Greek poets to show the way. In the 1857 edition, *Mnemosyna* consisted of ten poems: "Ode to Death," "The Slave Girl," "A Lullaby," "Thanasis Vayias," "Dimos and his Gun," "Kitzos and the Hawk," "Samuel," "Katsandonis," "The Flight," and "Efthymios Vlachavas." "The Laurel and the Nightingale," composed on the occasion of the death of Solomos in 1857, was added to the edition of 1867, though it differs from the others in both theme and structure. The poems will be discussed in the above order, without any attempt to pinpoint the exact dates of composition.

"Ode to Death," the first poem in this collection, is a simple lyric written in fresh and unpretentious language. It is the first poem Valaoritis wrote in the demotic. The poet expresses his puzzlement and sorrow over the death of the rose tree:

> One morning, with the dew, the rose tree sprang,
> On the next morning the rose tree died. . . .

Death becomes a recurrent theme from now on in the poetry of Valaoritis. The poet will find passionate words to lament the fact of death, which comes to all, to a rose bush as well as to a young captain who prefers torture and death rather than live without freedom. Death in this early poem is a phantom, an apparition, barely perceived at night while riding his horse along the sea shore:

> In his hand he held a faded rose,
> As he asked the wave: "Isn't my rose pretty?
> Am I not, too, worthy of wearing it?
> Such roses beautify even my own ugly breast,
> Believe me! Believe me!"

Death is cruel, but also morbidly fond of young and beautiful creatures, whom he pursues with special malevolence.

Interestingly, this poem does not have the explicitly patriotic theme of the other poems of this collection; but in a broader sense it symbolizes all innocent creatures marked to die, among them the young Greek hero who fights for liberty.

"The Slave Girl" adds little that is memorable to this group of poems. Both the subject matter and the imagery are patently melodramatic and conventional. A Greek slave girl is sending a dove with a message to her betrothed, Lambros, a freedom fighter in the mountains, asking him to rescue her from her captors. She is pining away in bondage, standing at her window and uttering laments for her misfortune. The poem is written in alternating lines of iambic tetrameter and trimeter, with short cadences that give the verse a tone of passionate tenderness. The images are vivid but only evoke stock responses: lightning is threatening the dove in its flight, the waves of the sea are about to swallow it up; the tears of the girl drop profusely over the written message. The poem has the pastoral tone typical of the popular songs, especially those describing the life of the mountaineer, the freedom-loving life of the klephts.

The next poem, "A Lullaby," is again in tetrameter, with some longer rhyming lines. It verges on the sentimental but at the same time it has lilt, showing that Valaoritis could write fresh, unpretentious lines on occasion. A widow is singing her young child to sleep; she is poor, works hard to make a living, and often prays to the Madonna to protect her child from evil. In its simplicity, the song of the mother has pathos and charm:

> Blow, cool breeze
> Through the leaves of trees,
> Take the bloom of the rose,
> The apple's blossom from the appletree,
> And bring them to my young one!

The babe's innocence, the mother's anguished care, idyllic pictures of peace and calmness, are interrupted by a shadow of lurking evil:

> Dreams are the hope of the poor,
> The widow's company, the sun, the light. . . .

The mother and child finally go to sleep. The poet blesses their calm and quiet. In a final line, he curses those who would dare look "with a cold eye" upon the mother and child.

"Thanasis Vayias" is the first important poem in *Mnemosyna,* and is one of Valaoritis' most celebrated. It is based on the legend of a traitor, Thanasis Vayias, a man who allegedly led the hordes of Ali Pasha against a village of Epirus, Gardiki, resulting in the massacre of seven hundred men, women, and children.[8] Though some critics have disputed Valaoritis' damaging verdict on Vayias, it is quite apparent that the poet did not pass judgment lightly. He had made his usual research with the then available sources and had concluded on the best historical evidence of his time that Vayias was indeed responsible for the slaughter at Gardiki and was a despicable and damnable figure.[9]

Valaoritis had, of course, a special abhorrence for traitors, as he had a love of brave warriors, and presented the two categories of men in vividly contrasting colors. Vayias is one in a series of portraits of traitors in Greek history going all the way back to Ephialtes, the man who betrayed Leonidas at Thermopylae. Vayias, Pilios Gousis, Gogos, the priest who betrayed Katsandonis, the traitor who leads the army of Vrionis in *Diakos*—all these are Greeks who turned against their own, giving an unfair advantage to vast numbers of enemy troops warring against the brave but tiny bands of Greek patriots. As a character, the traitor was stigmatized forever in poetry as well as folk memory; no forgiveness was possible, on earth or in heaven.

Valaoritis was not interested in a psychoanalytic portrayal of the motives of the traitor, and in his preface he admits that the poem has no other function than to cast another stone in the general condemnation of Vayias. The poet must not be expected to be humane here. Vayias emerges as a symbol, not a real human being. Further, the poem narrates the actions of Vayias after his death. It follows the fate of his widow, who, hungry and in rags, wanders from door to door begging for bread and shelter. One stormy night she knocks on the door of a poor Christian woman who lives in a hut with her only daughter. The traitor's widow cries for help, and half dead is dragged inside and given refuge from the storm. But she cannot go to sleep, for the ghost of Vayias, her husband, visits her.

The ghost—*vrykólakas* or *phántasma*—is a familiar figure in modern Greek demonology. It can be anywhere at night, and even during the afternoon hours, when everyone is taking the customary nap, it roams from cemeteries to narrow village streets, deserted houses, churchyards, or under fig trees. It is not particularly bloodthirsty, like its Transylvanian counterpart, Count Dracula. It can be exorcised easily with two sticks of wood crossed together, the sign of the cross on one's breast, a few standard prayers, or even by turning on the lights. Domesticated, it sometimes becomes a convenient means for mothers to terrorize their children into eating their dinners or going to bed on time.

Valaoritis has, of course, described this figure in its most hideous aspects, borrowing imagery abundantly from Dante and the English Gothic tradition. ("Vayias" was effectively translated into French and Italian.) Thanasis, the ghost, smells like a rotting corpse, bits of flesh are dropping from his bones, his eyes are holes, worms are eating at his face. His figure has suffered an allegorical transformation, what John Ciardi has called "symbolic retribution," a Dantean device for the punishment of sinners. There is a reversal of the nature of Vayias' crime; the victims of Vayias, the dead men of Gardiki he helped massacre, left their graves and, led by an infernal owl that distinctly cries out his name, came and dug up his corpse, "like mad dogs" from his grave. They pulled him up, dragged him to the scene of the crime,

> Shrouds sailing in the wind,
> Bones cracking to bits and falling,

where they subjected him to retributive punishment:

> Oh, what torture, oh, what horrors!
> What curses didn't they hurl at me!
> Jelled blood I was given to drink,
> Here, look how my mouth is stained. . . .

After the dead finally departed, Vayias remained alone. He now comes to his wife, seeking her company for succor, for sexual pleasure. He begs for a kiss—she is repelled. He insists, attacks her, tears her clothes away, fondles her bosom—suddenly he stops, petrified, "his jaws shaking." He has touched the "honored wood," a talisman she wears containing a piece of wood from the cross of Christ. This saves her; the ghost vanishes.

This poem, singled out by some critics as a Valaoritis masterpiece, has also been regarded as one of the poet's most popular. The element of horror, the vivid imagery, the quick alterations of scenery and staccato rhythm, the melodramatic action, the theatrical and sensational tone make this an interesting intermixture of styles; romantic melodrama and imagery fitted into the patriotic mold—the martyrdom of Greece under the Turkish yoke and the traitor's crime and punishment. But despite its overt allegory, the poem does not achieve the heights of symbolic significance, as "Astrapoyiannos" and *Athanasis Diakos* do. Still, this poem shows Valaoritis' enormous capacity for theatrical display of emotions and his talent for composing fast-moving, arresting verse.

"Dimos and his Gun," written with the simplicity and economy of the klephtic songs, relates an old warrior's yearning for death and repose. The proud old man, having lived an active life as a klepht in the Greek mountains for fifty years, is now preparing to give up the spirit. Calm and clearheaded, he gives his young comrades instructions for burial:

> If over my grave a plane tree grows, let
> The young come under it and hang their weapons;
> If a cypress, dark and lovely, let them come
> And take my apples and dress their wounds and
>   bless the soul of Dimos. . . .

When he is dead, he wants the youngest of the men to take his gun, "the worthy karyofilli," climb to the mountain top, and fire three blasts, crying each time: " 'Old Dimos is dead, old Dimos is gone!' " This, Dimos believes, will ensure his place with the immortals. For though he is dead, his spirit will live on to nourish the souls of his younger companions and urge them to comparable acts of heroism. When the gun explodes for the third time, he will smile in his sleep, content, for, "The brave man's death gives fresh life to youth."

Valaoritis has captured here the image of the klepht in its purest simplicity and vigor. For the first time, he uses the fifteen-syllable line, the verse medium of the popular klephtic ballads, without rhyme. This makes the line terser, more vigorous, and less pretentious than in the previous poems. The poem is one of the most memorable of its kind and has been repeatedly set to music.

"Kitzos and the Hawk" is another poem based on the popular song formula, but it is more diffuse than "Dimos," more conventional in its imagery and technique, lacking the memorable lines and situation of the previous poem. Kitzos, an old warrior, is sitting on a rock facing Kiapha, one of the villages that held heroically against Ali Pasha, but which finally succumbed and was razed. A hawk flying above hears his groans and stops momentarily to talk to him and divert him from his sorrow. The rest of the poem is a dialogue between the two. This form is typical of many of Valaoritis' poems and has the basic structure of the folk songs. The hawk is, of course, a symbol of freedom, and a messenger from those who have died for Greece. It talks to Kitzos in a human voice, urging him to climb to the mountaintops to hear the cries of warriors fighting for liberty elsewhere. "Who are you?" asks the klepht, amazed. "How come you have a human voice?" "I am the soul of Rhigas,"[10] replies the bird, busily flying away to carry the news of the Greek uprising to Europe, the heathen Europe that once crucified him. The poem ends with a rhetorical reassurance on the part of the poet that Greece will, indeed, be resurrected.

"Samuel," the next poem, is a tribute to the famous monk at Koughi, a rocky outpost of Suli, who blew himself up with his companions rather than surrender to the hordes of Veli, the son of Ali Pasha. This is one of the most admired figures in the pantheon of the Valaoritis heroes, a man who combined the dual roles of priest and fighter. Valaoritis had special esteem for such men and saw nothing contradictory in the roles they could be called upon to play under unusual circumstances.

Freedom was a God-given gift and had to be defended at all costs. Opportunity to fight presented the priest with a useful role, and his presence on the battlefield indicated holy sanction, insuring forgiveness for the sin of killing for the participants. As we shall see later, *Diakos* was the supreme example of this type of hero.

At the beginning of the action, Samuel is still fighting inside Koughi, the impregnable fort built on a steep rock. But only five men have been left him, and he is running out of ammunition. Determined to stay to the last, he rejects the ignominious proposals for surrender made by Pilios Gousis, a traitor, who is shouting the orders of Veli from outside. Inside the fort, in the tiny chapel, the fighters are kneeling before the Holy Porte. They all prepare to take communion, expecting to fight to the last and die. They are hungry, their tongues parched with thirst. Not a drop of water is available for the priest to perform the sacrament. Samuel apologizes to God, offering his tears as libation. The old man appears through the porte, his face "luminous like a snowy peak with moonlight on it." His arms embrace the last keg of gunpowder. He kneels before the Holy Table, "his knees striking the stone." He offers a lengthy prayer, a lament for those who died defending Suli, and he vows to sacrifice himself too. Then he blesses his companions and administers communion. As he sings, the noise, clatter, and footsteps of the invading enemy are heard. He drops a spark from the candle on the gunpowder, and all, Samuel, his men, and the oncoming enemy, are blown up.

The poem ends with a striking scene, a typical resolution of most Valaoritic tragedies. The priest's robe is now flying upward, and, growing larger and more ominous as it travels, shades the light of the sun. Wherever it passes, it sets the heavens on fire, but finally brings rains to relieve the scorched land and regenerate the grass, the olive trees, and myrtles—symbols of joy, hope, and freedom.

With "Katsandonis" the heroic theme continues. Katsandonis, a legendary prerevolutionary chieftain living around 1780, fought against Ali, performing deeds of incredible daring and bravery. But he was stricken with an infectious disease (possibly smallpox) and retreated to a remote cave in the mountains tended by his brother and a priest, who brought him provisions. The priest turned traitor and Katsandonis was arrested by Ali's bravos as he and his brother attempted to escape. Both men were brought to Jannina, where they were tortured and executed.

The poem, consisting of eighty lines of rhyming fifteen-syllable couplets, begins *in medias res*, with the capture and execution of Katsandonis. Employing a device used frequently in popular songs, the poet first asks the wild birds sailing over the mountain-tops—eagles, hawks, and swallows—to weep for the captured hero. Then, the poet fiercely denounces the traitor, shrilly cursing and piling anathemas on him and his like.

Then we are told of the flight of the two brothers from the cave, of the heroism of Giorgos, who tries to carry the ailing hero away on his shoulders while wounded himself, and of their final capture. At Jannina, under a plane tree, "The blood-dripping Golgotha of heroes," the executioners are waiting. Their tools are burning wood sticks, hammers, an anvil. The two brothers look into each other's eyes for a moment, re-membering their past youth and feats of bravery. A blade shines, Giorgos is decapitated with one blow. "Christ is Risen!" cries Andonis. His brother's soul will not depart, however, but hides in the plane tree and watches the other brother's torture. Andonis is killed slowly; all his bones are broken one by one. The scene is one of horror and Valaoritis describes it in vivid detail:

> The splintered bones go flying, marrow scatters,
> Shredded nerves, mangled flesh, chopped to bits—
> But he looks toward heaven and sings sweetly. . . .

Finally, the executioners slit their victim's throat, but still the words gurgle out hoarsely:

> Strike me, chop me, kill me,
> Nothing frightens Andonis,
> No fire, no hammer, no anvil. . . .

The blood sinks down into the plane tree's roots; the tree soaks it up greedily; it grows gigantic, with monstrous branches which will soon haunt and terrify Ali in his dreams. The poem ends on an allegorical note. The branches are the souls of the dead heroes, who will one day avenge the cruelty of the tyrant and help liberate Greece.

"The Flight" is one of the best known of Valaoritis' poems, and to this day is frequently recited in high school ceremonies and on patriotic occasions. It is one of the few still admired by today's critics.[11] It tells of the flight of Ali Pasha from a battle with the famous chief of the Suliotes, Lambros Tjavellas. The success of the poem lies mainly in its powerful verse. Abandoning the somewhat cumbersome fifteen-syllable line, Valaoritis uses the lighter meter of the eleven-syllable dactylic line to render the beat of the hoofs of the retreating horse, thus creating an atmosphere of breathless motion, representing a mind seized by fear and panic.

The poem opens with a memorable scene: Ali Pasha, the awesome tyrant of Jannina, has just lost the battle and is frantically looking about for a means of escape. "A horse, a horse!" he shouts to his second in command. "A horse, Omer Vrioni, Suli is out to capture me!"

The poem is a variation of the familiar topic: the tyrant is depicted as cruel or cowardly, while the fighter for liberty is a man valiant in battle, brave and persevering when captured and tortured. As he mounts his noble horse, described in four stanzas of powerful and evocative verse, the terrified Ali sees the shadow of Tjavellas everywhere. He gallops away in a frenzied flight, and, when the horse stumbles, beats the animal without mercy until it collapses in exhaustion. Mad with fury, "He plants two bullets into its ear-root." Half dead, a distraught, humiliated Ali manages to reach Jannina, but the specter of Tjavellas haunts him for a long time.

Extravagant in both imagery and tone, the poem successfully exploits the means of expressionistic art—sound effects, rhythmic devices to suggest speed, suspense, and tension in recreating the moment of panic. But it falls short of making a statement, except perhaps in an indirect way: the poet has expressed his contempt for Ali's cowardice, while the hero, Lambros, is admired. The poem, however, is not to be reflected upon, but to be read aloud or recited to an audience.

"Efthimios Vlachavas" is the most ambitious poem in the collection, but, at the same time, the least successful. Consisting of approximately 290 fifteen-syllable lines, it is loose in structure, exhibiting the usual defects of verbosity and a lack of control of the subject matter. It is too long for the incident it describes: it is divided into three parts and contains long declamatory speeches, stiff dialogue, and a torture scene that somehow lacks the crispness and directness of the one in "Katsandonis." At the same time, the poem, especially the opening chapter, has moments of beauty in its idyllic descriptions of nature and the Greek mountains, and the character of Vlachavas is drawn with commendable psychological insight, free from the usual patriotic stereotyping.

The introduction summarizes the birth and life of Efthimios Vlachavas, a legendary fighter of the prerevolutionary period who frequented the haunts of the mountains Olympus, Pindos, and Ossa. As no one knew the name of his parents, and because of his great bravery, it was rumored that Vlachavas had been begotten by Mount Olympus in a union with Ossa. Vlachavas roamed the plains of Thessaly, wreaking havoc upon the Turkish troops, being particularly bothersome to Ali, who had vowed revenge. Dimitrios, a learned monk, known for his devotion and piety, accompanied Efthymios in his adventures. "These two," comments Valaoritis in his introduction, "in the midst of wilderness, sitting under the shady trees, in the silence of the myrtle-fragrant Greek valleys, conceived the great idea of our national rising."[12] But their happy times did not last. The relentless Ali, always in pursuit, finally managed to wear them out and capture them, after a vast army of his had surrounded them at a lone outpost, where they had been abandoned by their companions. Vlachavas was dragged to Jannina, where he was put to painful tortures, while Dimitrios was placed alive inside a wall and left there to die.

The poem begins with an account of the legendary birth of the hero, an idyllic scene, reminiscent of Theocritus, in which lovelorn Mount Olympus (a masculine noun in Greek) courts Ossa (a feminine noun), a mountain less precipitous and more wooded than Olympus. The moment of the conception of

Vlachavas is a spring night, "when stars sparkle, and calm reigns, God's joy."

> A flock of sheep passes in the distance,
> Silence broken by bells ringing and bleatings.
> Laurel, myrtle smell sweetly; the lilacs peep
> Out of the water. All night the courtship lasts.
> And at dawn, when the morning star appears,
> Olympus stoops from his height and kisses Ossa.

Hardly any time goes by before a roar echoes throughout the mountains, the voice "of the terrifying Vlachavas, the awe-inspiring klepht."

But the heroic son, born in this mythical, almost Hesiodic manner, was not destined to live for long. His parents, old and snowy, hear the bitter news that their son has been captured by Ali's bravos.

The second section of the poem, "The Confession," is long-winded and generally inferior in composition. The tone, however, remains sublime. Efthimios, or "Thimios," as the poet now calls him, is in a deep sleep in his cell. He is chained and compelled to kneel on sharp flintstones. His torturers are asleep nearby, stretched on the ground, snoring, "like wolves whose lust for blood has been sated."

As he sleeps, Thimios sees a vision: Dimitrios, the monk, comes in to give him absolution. The image of the monk demands that it be recognized and heard. Thimios complains that his eyelids have been burned with hot iron; molten lead has been poured into his ears. A dog has come in with Dimitrios; Thimios pities the animal and begs his friend to feed him. The monk then asks Thimios to confess his sins, since this is the time to die. The prisoner hesitates for a moment: "Life, how beautiful! Why should it be given up? Why can't I live to see my country free? How lovely is Thessaly this time of year! Is that a sin, to love life?" he asks his confessor. The moment is highly dramatic, and classic in its simplicity. Thimios repeats the complaint of Antigone, who was also brave and unyielding until the time came for her to be taken to the cave. The heroes of Valaoritis love life's beauty intensely and passionately especially at the moment they must give it up for a higher purpose.

Thimios bends and confesses before the severe monk, who replies that love of life is no sin, but, "It would be a sin not to forgive your enemies." Thimios finds the command hard to obey. But confronted with the prospect of becoming a sinner and a rebel against God, he forgives his torturers. The scene is quite memorable and forceful, revealing a degree of complexity in the delineation of character: "Forgiving is essential. Beside the deep river of the blood you have shed, this is a drop. Are you not satisfied yet? Who do you think you are, Vlachavas?" "I am the son of Olympus, don't you know me?" "Vlachavas, either forgive, or risk being excommunicated," the monk warns. Vlachavas relents immediately and pronounces his enemies forgiven. Communion is now administered. Thimios asks for a last favor: three golden hairs grow in his head; he asks the monk to pluck them out and take them to the mountains the hero had loved: " 'Let the mountains keep these as memory; let / Them not forget my manhood is in them.' " Thimios dies, and the monk leaves the cell as he came, imperceptibly.

The last section, "The Corpse," is forceful in parts, but on the whole diffuse and rather loose as composition. The bravos drag the body of Vlachavas through the streets of Jannina for three days. As the head bumps against the pavement stones, the three hairs, which have remained unplucked, are uprooted. The bravos finally sever the head from the body and place it high on a rock; the dog of Vlachavas takes the head and carries it to the mountains, where he buries it. On a future date, the "womb will open," and the hero's soul will leap out joyously: "The seed does not rot, buried in the snow, / No matter how deep buried it lies there now," is the poet's last lament, carrying its usual allegorical implications.

The last poem in the collection, "The Laurel and the Nightingale," written in honor of the death of Solomos, is a rather lengthy composition saying little that is either original or distinctive about Solomos. In a facile allegorical manner, Solomos is compared to a nightingale that has ceased to sing, while a laurel tree, the symbol of Greekness, is asked by the poet to

explain why her companion is absent. The laurel then is compared to a widow whose beloved has gone away. She is not
alone, however: the souls of the brave men who have sacrificed
their lives for freedom are also expecting to hear the song
of the nightingale which will have a regenerative effect on
them, as well as on all nature, and on every Greek soul. Finally,
the poet reviews the actions of the revolutionary heroes such
as Kanaris; Gregorios, the martyr; the fighters in the mountains
of Pindos and Epirus. Thirty years have passed since the
nightingale sang these glories. The cold bones are now in their
graves, with no messenger to call them to life and make them
rise again. And yet, who knows how many years from now, the
nightingale might be heard again, singing the song of resurrection on May Day!

Nothing personal is said in this poem about Solomos, who is
seen only as a symbol and is never mentioned by name. The
allegorical figures of the laurel and the nightingale, and their
juxtaposition as symbols in the national struggle, absorb the
main interest of the poet, who is more preoccupied with Greece's
freedom than with the poetic achievements of Solomos or his
personality. The death of a national figure is a mournful event
only insofar as it has deprived Greece of a voice that sang the
death of its heroes and the glories of its battles.

IV *Critique of* Mnemosyna

As we have seen, the bulk of the *Mnemosyna* is comprised
of poems with patriotic themes taken almost exclusively from
popular sources and traditions. Chronologically, nearly all these
poems refer to events which took place before the War of
Independence, 1821–1829; the action of most of the poems
takes place at Epirus, the rugged mountainous terrain that
became the seat of many significant prerevolutionary battles
of Greek chieftains against Turks and Albanians. Epirus was
the place where Ali Pasha, the tyrant of Jannina, perpetrated
some of the most savage crimes against the native populations—
sometimes with the cooperation of despicable traitors. Epirus
was also the hallowed graveyard of the brave men who fought
and died—some of them after having been captured and sub-

jected to cruel tortures by the tyrant. The poet's overt purpose was to praise these heroes, to celebrate the sacred memory of their death with his songs. The collection is offered in lieu of a memorial service. The poems are "threnodic elegies," according to Palamas.[13] Valaoritis makes his purpose clear in several notes, letters, and introductory remarks that accompany the larger poems.

The technique of most of the *Mnemosyna* poems closely resembles that of the folk songs. The poet uses the device of contrasts, casting into sharp relief opposing forces—the hero against the traitor, good against evil, freedom versus slavery, life against death. Simple allegories are frequently woven into these patterns: a rose is hope and beauty; a dove, a messenger from a slave bringing hope to a free man; a hawk, the spirit of a dead hero; a priest's robe becomes a shadow that heralds devastation to the oppressor; the plane tree at Jannina, perhaps one of the most potent of Valaoritis' symbols, grows into a monster that stifles the tyrant with its branches.

For the most part, Valaoritis uses the fifteen-syllable line of the folk songs. At first, Valaoritis imitates this line wholesale, making little effort to refine or embellish it. Some of his poems achieve a remarkable simplicity in this fashion. "Dimos and his Gun," for instance, is as nearly a folk poem as any of Valaoritis' compositions and is treated as such by the Greek people, who continue to sing it at celebrations and parties and regard it as a klephtic song of old. Valaoritis gradually became very conscious of his technique and for many years worked hard in perfecting the fifteen-syllable line, making it a terser and suppler vehicle of his long dramatic poems—*Diakos* and *Photeinos* in particular.

Valaoritis also worked with the shorter, eleven-syllable line (alternated frequently with a ten-syllable line), using it in iambic feet with trochaic or dactylic endings—a method that produces sound effects and quick changes of landscape and imagery. This device became the hallmark of certain popular pieces, such as "Thanasis Vayias," "The Flight," and "Astrapoyiannos," poems which are most successful when read aloud.

The close resemblance of the *Mnemosyna* poems to the popular songs of the countryside may have been the cause of some of their weaknesses. Most of the poems in the collection show the same impersonality that one finds in the folk songs and the same lack of a distinctive personal style. Other defects are an inherent naiveté, repetitiousness, and a loquacity which must be restrained in consciously composed poetry. Valaoritis in his early poems had not sufficiently detached himself from the mannerisms of the folk songs. As Palamas correctly observed, he was still "too near to the popular tracks, while attempting to carve out new roads to the slopes of the mountains of the Muses."[14] To free himself from the constraints of the popular songs, Valaoritis would have to seek larger themes, more complex situations, more spacious stories, and a clearer vision of the aims of his poetry. These things he did come upon as he contemplated the composition of the long and ambitious narrative poem, *Kyra Phrosyni.*

CHAPTER 4

Athanasis Diakos *and* Kyra Phrosyni–
The Epics of History

I *Introduction to* Kyra Phrosyni

VALAORITIS began the composition of *Kyra Phrosyni* (*Lady Phrosyni*) in 1857 while at Murano, Italy, where he was visiting his father-in-law. It took him nearly two years of hard labor to finish the poem, which he liked to believe was solidly based on historical evidence.[1] *Kyra Phrosyni* was published in Corfu in 1859, and was well received both at home and abroad.[2] The poem runs approximately 2,000 lines, mostly unrhyming fifteen-syllable lines, with occasional rhyming couplets and other metric variations, and is subdivided into four cantos of unequal length.[3] It is a mixture of narrative and dialogue, interrupted by short lyric passages and apostrophic speeches by the poet, and contains a brief "epic" catalogue at the beginning of the third canto describing captured Greek weapons hung on the walls of Ali Pasha.

With *Kyra Phrosyni*, Valaoritis attempts for the first time to define the larger aims of his own poetry, and at the same time to lay the foundations for modern Greek poetry in general. *Phrosyni*, he explains in a letter to Laskaratos, "is not a so-called romantic poem, and not an epic poem; nor is it tragic, but something new, something suited to my ideas and my imagination."[4] In writing it he did not wish to gather fame and glory for himself, but "to give relief to the aching of [his] heart, to offer a prayer for those dead who lie forgotten in their grassy tombs."[5] His would be "a poem with Greek character," and one that was "mainly historical."[6]

In his preface to the poem, Valaoritis further explains his intention that the writing of *Phrosyni* would help to define the

character and origin of modern Greek poetry. He has "an un-
shakable belief," he says, "that the foundation of modern Greek
poetry must be the accurate narration of the sufferings of the
Greek people in their unending struggle to shake off the foreign
rule."[7] Valaoritis considered history—particularly the period between the fall of Byzantium and the beginning of the War of
Independence, which may reasonably be called a "heroic"
period—to be the proper subject for Greek poetry. During this
time, Greece broke away from the Byzantine Empire, and
began to form a conscience and an identity of its own. "From
this moment on," the poet says, "the character of the modern
Greek nation is formed, and the prospects for its future begin
to develop. Greek poetry, therefore, at least in its formative
stages, must assume a heroic—that is, an epic—character, before
it turns to lyric and dramatic forms. And epic poetry means
chiefly poetry which, independently of certain rules, rests mainly
upon history."[8]

Events connected with the heroic times, such as those found
in the pages of chroniclers and the memories of the old, are
the most suitable for this type of poetry. Though the poet
must know all the available facts in order to make history the
basis of his poetry, he need not be overly concerned with
rendering accurate historical truth. The poet does not attempt
to narrate events in a chronological sequence, as the historian
does. During the four centuries of slavery, "events were more
or less identical, periods succeeded one another with uniformity,
epochs merged, intervals of time disappeared. Heroes of different
generations lived and fought as if they were contemporaries.
This page of Greek history is really one period, moving on a
parabolic line from the beginning to the end and back to the
beginning."[9] The poet should care little whether his subject
matter comes from the tenth or the nineteenth century as long
as its character is appropriate to his purpose.

The story on which the plot of *Kyra Phrosyni* is based is
quite suitable for this type of composition. Around the turn
of the century (1801), Ephrosyni, or Phrosyni, a lady of great
beauty and elegant manners but of loose moral conduct, created
a scandal by becoming the mistress of Mouhtar, the son of the
powerful Ali Pasha, the governor of Jannina. During her hus-

band's prolonged absences, the house of Phrosyni became the resort of handsome young men and other fair ladies of the city; she herself received visits and gifts from Mouhtar without attempting to conceal the disgraceful relationship. Presumably in reaction to citizens' complaints, but actually because he himself fell in love with her, Ali visited the beauteous Phrosyni pretending to be interested in her welfare. But when the sly old man declared his passion for her, she turned him down indignantly. Ali then had her and seventeen other young Greek women arrested and executed by drowning in the waters of the Lake of Jannina, offering the excuse that he had to protect the honor of outraged citizens.[10]

To Valaoritis, Phrosyni represented perfectly the symbol of Greekness. Like Greece, she was initially "pure and unspoiled," but, like her, she was dazzled by the conqueror's glamor, succumbed to temptation, and lost her honor. But she was capable of redemption. When the supreme test came, she realized her error, repented, and, through sacrifice, cleansed herself.

Ali Pasha, on the other hand, is the symbol of the Turkish Empire—"old, proud, and decaying," but still capable of delivering a blow to the rising young Hellas. Valaoritis studied the figure of Ali with unremitting interest throughout his life, and made him a leading character in many of his poems. His vision of him was historically well documented, but in the poem historical considerations are frequently set aside and Ali becomes a mythical villain, larger than life, a providential monster meant to be the nemesis of erring Greeks. He persecuted warriors without pause, torturing those he captured, murdering all those that stood in his path. He was, in the words of Valaoritis, "a destructive flood that swept everything in its passage." On his face was stamped the image of the Ottoman Empire, "old now, but still preserving all its organic elements. He was the last nail in the Greek crucifixion."[11]

But Valaoritis saw the tyrant as also serving an important function in the drama of Greece. Through him, the Greeks obtained the catharsis of their own sins and weaknesses. Phrosyni's seduction by Mouhtar—"This monstrous and symbolic mixture," as Valaoritis puts it—"is also symbolic of the Greek situation in a broader sense."[12] The Greeks had not always been steadfast in the pursuit of their national destiny. Many young warriors—among whom were Athanasis Diakos and Odysseus Androutsos—had been attracted by Ali's promises of collaboration to overthrow the sultan and trained in his military camps for years. But when Ali used these warriors to advance his own schemes and intrigues, often setting them against one another, they, like Phrosyni, became aware of their duty and the necessity of sacrifice for their country's liberation. They left his camp and joined the forces of the chieftains of Sterea Hellas at the outbreak of the war. Some of them, as in the case of Athanasis Diakos, met a martyr's death. Thus, unwittingly, Ali had turned into an instrument "that washed and cleansed the Greek race of its impurities."[12]

II *Plot Summary of* Kyra Phrosyni

Canto I. "The Mystery." The poem begins with a peaceful description of Jannina, the capital of Epirus, where Ali, the Albanian satrap, reigns. Night has fallen, and all are in bed asleep. Mothers clutch their children dearly to their breasts, for these are hard times and evil seems to be hanging over the land. Not a sound is heard, all is calm and quiet, not a soul breathes a word. Sleep is like death, beds like tombs. With his characteristic turn of phrase, the poet describes the country "as a cemetery, with night its lone chapel."

Only Ali is staying up, sleepless, stretched on a lionskin, his forehead clouded with thoughts. He is leaning on his elbow, his fingers stroking the snow white beard that hangs over his frightful chest. Near him stands Tahir, his faithful adviser, chief of police, and executioner. It is to him that Ali always confides his secret schemes and intrigues. But tonight Tahir finds his master's long silence disturbing. Is it perhaps the moonless night that has affected him? he asks discreetly. A storm is coming from behind the calm—has that spoiled the master's mood? Ali chides Tahir for having not yet realized that Ali's life itself is a storm, an ever dark winter with thunder and lightning. He is growing old, but he has not yet known peace and tranquility. Is this then the night to fear a storm, a few black clouds, the howling winds and darkness in the mountains? Has Tahir grown weak and fearsome? "Then, you should join my son, Mouhtar, for company," adds Ali sarcastically.

Tahir hurries to beg his master's pardon. Has he ever failed to execute an order, or to carry out a plan, no matter what it was? "Tell me what you want," he says, "and I will do it for you. We two, united, can destroy the beauty of the world." Ali then delivers a long, passionate speech in which he laments the loss of his youth, but not the loss of his desires. His heart still beats madly in his chest, his blood boils; he can still love, but young women detest his hoary appearance. Though he has a whole harem of young slave girls, he is not happy to have to beg for their charms. Tahir will have to save him from this humiliation.

Tahir replies with an equally long speech with numerous elaborate metaphors ("you are the blade, I am the scabbard"), reminding Ali of their past adventures, the blood they shed together as they dominated the world. He is amazed to hear Albania's fearless lion sigh like a lovelorn partridge. Ali came from a poor family of low origin; he hated the world, but managed to subdue it. Tahir reassures his master once more of his devotion, stating that he is ready to commit any act, to bring to him any woman or child of Jannina to please him.

Ali is glad that Tahir remembers the past so well. The memories of blood, murder, and graveyards refresh his heart. Ali did not come into this world to love God's creatures, or His image. He was begotten by another God, one who taught him that his life is "black death and hell" here on earth. He remembers the time when, while he was still a boy, his mother took him away from his brothers to a place "where many tombs shone under the moonlight." A gigantic dark cypress rose alone above the tombs. It was a quiet night, with only the cry of the wolf being heard in the distance. There, his mother, Hamko, initiated him into the practice of evil. Hamko's instructions were infernal: no one suffers in the tomb, she said, no children cry there. Blessed is he who, instead of planting new life into a woman's flesh—where dragons and lions and snakes are born— "digs deep into the earth and buries bodies; no matter how evil these have been, they will bring forth roses, fruits, flowers, green grass."

"If you want your mother's blessing," Hamko said, "remember to be a good father, and make the bed for your children and put them to sleep." Hamko called his attention to the dark cypress standing above the graves: "Do you see its shadow, passing over the marble tombstones, like a hand, counting the hours? As you are going into the world, become a cypress, and count your hours, years, your life by spreading your shadow over the cold tombs." Thus Hamko counselled her son—with a curse pending should he disregard her words. "I conquered the world that night," Ali observes, still elated over the recollection of his mother's words.

But now he has been seized by a passion, a strange thirst is burning him. If he knew he could quench it by drinking blood, he would kill his entire Albanian army—even Tahir himself! His secret is great, unspeakable! Yes, Tahir, he says, the fearless lion, the tameless wolf is eaten up by jealousy! "Put your hand here, measure the wound in my heart," exclaims Ali theatrically. "Pity me!"

Tahir assures him that passion and jealousy are signs of youth. Love shows that a man is still young. Tahir, who exhibits a pathological devotion for Ali, says he will shed his blood, if need be, to serve his master: "I would cut my own throat, kill my own child, and bring you his blood to drink, visier, my father," he cries. Ali then confesses that he is magnetized by the beauty of Phrosyni, the loveliest woman at Jannina. In a lyric passage showing Ali a man of romantic contrasts, the poet describes Phrosyni's dazzling beauty, which, like a fleeting vision, remains uncaptured:

> ... He stretched his hand to catch her, but
> she always fled, like foam between the
> sailor's fingers, thinking he grasps the
> shore's rocks, the life-giving.

Ali knows that Phrosyni had left her husband and her two little children and now has a lover. Tahir wants to know the lover's name; Ali hesitates for a moment, then reveals it—it is Mouhtar, his own son! Tahir turns pale, deeply shocked. "Your own child?" he mumbles. "This is the last time I hear you say such things," Ali thunders. "My child! I have no children, I am no father, not me!" He has a plan: he will send Mouhtar away to a war; then Tahir and he together will go to visit Phrosyni the following night. Ali drops a hint that, since now he has no other son, Tahir might be the one to take his place should something happen to Mouhtar. Tahir, who is no novice in the business of crime, shudders to hear Ali harboring such monstrous thoughts. Still, he is obedient. Stooping, he kisses Ali's hand, touches his knife, and bowing three times goes out of the room.

Alone now, Ali blasphemes, defying God. He owes his strength to no one. He challenges God to show his strength to him in any way He chooses. He is aware that his mission of bringing evil into the world will be defeated. Age is catching up with him; day by day he loses ground. He feels as if he were struck by a hidden, invisible power. His challenge is itself an admission of his defeat. But Ali has not given up; he still rejects God, His world, and all those cowards who are afraid to deny Him. He believes in Him only because he intends to fight Him! But let God be fair, let Him give Ali his youth back, so that the fighting forces might be equal! In a fury of bombastic rhetoric, Ali raves maliciously, declaring that he will steal Phrosyni just to show God he is capable of stifling any human feelings.

Canto II. "The Repentance." This canto opens with a lyric description of the Lake of Jannina. It is early dawn; dew has fallen from the Pindos Mountains, "sprinkling dawn's steps." The lake is asleep, tranquil; on the edge of the shore wavelets break, making a whisper like a child's quiet breath. Suddenly, the mist lifts, flying upwards like sacred incense, revealing the beauty of the lake. The symbolism of the scene is obvious: the lake is innocence; its purity is hidden at night by the mist which, lifting in the morning, rises to the feet of God to remind Him of enslaved Epirus.

A sentimental description of Phrosyni follows. She is standing at her window, heartbroken, her hair loose, weeping for the departure of her beloved Mouhtar. There is a lengthy scene of diffuse lamentation, during which Phrosyni alternately misses her lover, or is stricken by remorse as she remembers the abandoment of her own little children.

Consoled somewhat by the presence of her faithful nurse, Chrysis, Phrosyni passes a tormented day of remorse and anguish. Finally, night comes and she falls asleep exhausted; it is almost morning when a ferocious knock comes on the door. Terrified, she awakens to find Ali standing at her side. His face is on fire, his eyes glistening and rolling in their sockets. He sees her in bed, alone, and he is consumed with lust: " . . . He smiles, and his teeth shine white / in his broad mouth, greedy like the soil." Never before did his heart beat so madly, threatening to break his ribcage. He breathes heavily, his chest heaving sighs, one after another. He stretches his hand toward her, "His fingers sliding like snakes." She kneels before him. "Don't hurt a helpless woman dragging herself before your feet, mighty visier," she pleads. "Wherever you step, the ground crumbles—your step breaks rocks. I am a little dust carried away by the wind. Have pity on me, visier, don't crush me."

This passionate plea is given forcefully, and Phrosyni is suddenly transformed into a real person. She is no longer the whimpering lovelorn lady of the previous scene, but a woman determined to save her honor. Ali hesitates for a moment, seemingly touched by her words. The horrible sin of what he is about to do torments him, "gnawing his insides." He turns and beckons to Tahir, who has also entered and is standing by the door. The latter understands instantly, and goes out taking Chrysis with him. The monster then kneels and confesses to Phrosyni. He claims that he loves her like a father, and he asks her to find solace in his embrace. He threatens to kill whoever brought sorrow to her. Why doesn't she lean on his paternal bosom, telling him her sorrows? "Let me wipe your tear-drenched hair with my hands," the diabolical old man says.

She believes his words and kisses his hand, resting her head against his chest. But his hands creep slowly over her bosom, and she feels his burning breath; she tries to escape, but he is already kissing her madly. She leaps away, "like a doe feeling in her side the hunter's bullet." He kneels before her and confesses his love with the fury and passion of a Volpone or a Tartuffe—two hypocritical impostors of large dimensions whom

he resembles. His love is all-consuming, carrying him to heights
—almost for a moment redeeming him.

> My life, my riches are yours, take them,
> I ask you for nothing else, my Phroso,
> But let this old man sit in your shade
> Once in a while, my pretty little tree!
> . . . .
> Pity me! Pity me! Oh, there is a God
> If a beauty like you does exist!

But Phrosyni stands firm, unshaken and fearless before him.
Her resistance is a blow to his ego; it shatters his illusion of
power. He begins to rant, threatening her with death, claiming
to have the power of God. He lies to her, pretending that
Mouhtar instructed him before his departure to take Phrosyni
for a lover. But Phrosyni answers defiantly, calling him a "snake"
and a "murderer." He begs her for a kiss, she refuses; they
struggle, "two elements, crime and innocence," says the poet
somewhat simplistically. The bay leaves from the icon of the
Virgin, hanging on the wall above, fall on the tyrant's head,
and he retreats in horror. But again he attacks, laboring to obtain
a kiss. She shakes him loose once more. He runs after her, over-
throws the icon of the Virgin, blasphemes—the candle goes out.
Phrosyni uses this as an opportunity to run away from him
and grab a knife; when Ali recovers, she is standing before him
shouting, ready to stab him. Ali creeps away "like a scorpion,"
frightened. He finds the door and slips out into the night. He
calls the guards; they come near and see Phrosyni holding the
knife. Shouting that he has been attacked, he commands them
to arrest her. The verdict is pronounced quickly: she will be
drowned in the lake with sixteen other young women, all
newlyweds. Ali gives instructions that she must be treated gently,
for, after all, she is his son's mistress! Then he flies, his tongue
dripping bile, his step scaring all creeping things from his
path. He reaches his palace, sprawls on his bed, and remains
in a sleepless torpor for the rest of the night.

    Canto III. "The Day of Judgment." When morning arrives,
Ali awakes from a bad night, looking whiter, older. He has

failed to recapture his youth by courting and winning the young and beautiful woman; Phrosyni has rejected him, and he feels the pain keenly. He is a horrifying spectacle to behold. His bravos, Veli-Gekas and Jusuf-Arapi, stand before him, trembling with terror; Tahir as always is standing a little to the side. They know Ali's temper and they are awaiting a storm.

High on Ali's walls hang the weapons of the Greek fighters captured by the tyrant at different times. These come from famous chieftains—men like Millionis, Boukouvallas, Stathas, Zithros, and others. Pistols, blades, rifles "Are hanging idle, decorating a dead wall." The poet wants these weapons "freed" and fighting in the mountains where their masters fought and died. This is one of the best written passages in the poem, and one of the few digressions leading away from the main story to its overlapping theme—that the oppressed will soon rise to throw off the yoke of the oppressor, making restitution for the blood now being shed. It is during the time of the uprising, "twenty short years from now," that the idle weapons will resound again throughout the mountains of Epirus.

The scene shifts to the city. The flowers in the flowerpots are withering everywhere, presumably because the young women are in prison and no one is there to water them. Dew falls from the sky and revives them somewhat. Songs, laughter, pipers playing are heard from the gypsy quarters of the palace: these are slaves who dance on order, as if with the pretense of joy they could stifle their fears. At the service of Ali, the gypsies kill, torture, dismember prisoners. Scenes of horror are everyday occurrences; even small children play with skulls—building pyramids. These are the bravos and executioners of Ali, men selected for their cruelty, accustomed to the art of torture, impervious to human suffering. As an old man passes by, begging for alms, the insolent pranksters find an opportunity for fun: they place a piece of flesh from a corpse and a live coal in his open palm; then, they kick him away, laughing coarsely. The poet vents his indignation at this point, with a classic line— "Jannina, dark Jannina, how does this earth bear you!" reminiscent of Dante's "O Pisa, vituperio delle genti!"

The scene shifts back to the palace, where Ali orders his guards to bring in Drakos, an old warrior who was captured

with two of his men during the night. The old klepht enters, and
Valaoritis describes him in impressive lines:

> The old man stands straight like a cypress;
> Years have not bent his ferocious neck;
> His snow white mane creeps to his loins,
> And his naked chest shines dark and bushy;
> His eyes are the eagle's, his forehead a rock—
> Where brows like ivy have taken root. . . .

When Drakos sees the captured arms hanging on Ali's walls,
he lets a tear drop. "Blessed tear," interjects the poet.

Ali scowls at the old man, trying to bully him into submission. But Drakos, whose name is symbolic of his virtue
(*drakos* means dragon), defies the tyrant, refusing to obey
his order and kneel before him. Ali promises to pardon him,
if he will change his faith and enlist in his service. But the old
klepht rejects the offer scornfully, and Ali orders his men to
take him away and have his bones broken with hammers, the
usual torture. As the old warrior is taken out, he sings a song
of liberty: "For forty years I have fought the Turks. . . ."

Tahir appears, announcing that the seventeen women are in
prison, and that everything is ready to proceed with the execution. Ali inquires whether Phrosyni wept when she was captured.
No, she showed exceptional courage, Tahir replies with evident
admiration.

Upon hearing this, Ali feels envy: Phrosyni is suffering her
fate with complete equanimity, rising above him. But envy
gives way to admiration as Ali waxes lyrical, entranced by the
vision of a beauteous young woman going to her martyrdom
without bending. But she has offended him and she must die.
Quickly, he gives orders to Tahir how the seventeen young
women are to be drowned in the lake. Torture is to be carefully
avoided, and their beauty must be preserved to the last. Ali is,
of course, not being compassionate; he simply wants to make
sure that if Phrosyni relents at the last moment and agrees to
become his mistress her beauty will remain unspoiled.

In the next scene, Ignatios, the bishop of Arta, enters the
palace, seeking to visit the imprisoned women and administer

the last rites. Ignatios commands the respect of all the chieftains of Pindos, and Ali has never dared to touch him. Ignatios pleads strongly for the release of the captive women. Haven't all the crimes of Ali against the Christians been enough? Ali, the Nero of modern times, has killed Turks and Christians alike on the slightest pretext. No one is left, the bishop moans. "You are left, and some others," Ali replies sullenly. His anger rising, Ignatios warns Ali that those who are left will soon deal with his insolent slaughters: "There is someone who can destroy even you." But knowing that the monster has no fear of mortals, Ignatios tries to cajole him into forgiving the seventeen condemned women. Again dissembling, Ali pretends to be a victim of circumstances: his destiny has doomed him to slaughter his own children. It's a bitter fate he has to suffer; he hopes that the seventeen women do not leave a curse upon him, Ignatios must see to that. (As he says this Ali wipes his eyes.) Terrified, Ignatios leaves without adding another word.

Canto IV. "The Litany." With a heavy heart Ignatios now descends into the cell where the condemned women are held prisoners. Behind him follows the deacon in silence, holding the holy sacraments. Smoke rises from the censer, symbolic of the same upward route that all these souls will take this night. The smell of incense reaches the world outside, bringing hushed prayers for the unlucky women to the lips of the people of Jannina.

Ignatios is led to the women, who eagerly flock around him, asking for his blessing. Phrosyni is standing to one side, fearful, conscious of her sin. Gently, Ignatios invites her to come near him, and she falls on her knees and confesses sincerely. It was Ignatios who raised her like a father, and she knows the shock he felt when he heard that she had left her husband and two little children to run away with a lover. Phrosyni humbly begs his forgiveness. Relentless, Ignatios reminds her in strong language that her sin is great, but when she begs for mercy, he finally forgives her. Ignatios then administers communion and instructs all the women to behave bravely and with dignity as the final hour approaches. Tahir appears at the door and commands the bishop to take his leave. Ignatios departs after

a brief farewell, and Tahir orders the women outside. They
leave the prison. The night air is cool, the dew falling; the
stars are bright, and the wind calm. The women walk silently
in a line, drinking the cool air greedily. Their eyes try to pierce
the darkness to see a familiar face, perhaps behind the few
windows that half open as they pass. They hear a subdued
sob occasionally, or a thin voice offering a blessing before it
fades away.

Phrosyni walks last; she is pale and weak from suffering.
Tahir asks her with fake compassion whether she would like
to sit down and rest for a while; he tries to make her speak
to him, talk to him of her troubles. What a pity, he drones on,
that such a great beauty as hers is soon to vanish in the waters
of the lake. If she would only change her mind and listen to
the counsel of the visier, who desires nothing but her own
good! Phrosyni prays, begging the Virgin to keep her strong
in her resolution. Tahir persists, using soft, persuasive words,
pretending affection and understanding. In cunning and powers
of dissimulation, Tahir is the exact duplicate of his master,
and he takes pleasure in torturing Ali's victims. In a lyrical
outburst he describes the beauty of nature, pointing to the
blooming oleander and citrus trees as they pass through the
park; why should she forsake this beauteous sight, exchanging
it for the coldness of the tomb? Seeing her still unwavering,
Tahir uses the last, most powerful temptation: he reminds her
of her children, who will soon be orphans, sadistically describing
them as they will be when their mother is gone. But Phrosyni
continues to stand firm. She even declines his offer to take a
drink of water and quench her thirst; she will have plenty of
that soon enough, she says. Tahir gnashes his teeth furiously,
moaning so loudly that the women shudder with terror.

As they walk, Tahir's eyes catch a shadow behind a bush;
it is Ali, holding the two frightened children of Phrosyni, urging
them to cry out to their mother. The pitiful creatures cry out,
calling her by name. Phrosyni recognizes their voices; a sharp
pain stabs her heart and she drops to the ground, unconscious.
Ali leaps from behind the bush and commands Tahir to revive
her by any means; it's impossible that she has expired; she
must be kept alive to be drowned in the lake. He asks Tahir

whether she has shed any tears. "Not one," says Tahir. A faint moan comes from the lips of the corpse. Believing she is still alive, Ali orders Tahir to take her to the lake immediately.

The other women are waiting. Three or four of the executioners, who had spent the night there, help load the young women on the boat. With a nod from Tahir, the men strike the oars and the boat vanishes into the night. Ali listens from the shore. When he hears the first splash he smiles, and begins to count. A second, a third comes—he keeps counting. A few more are left; "The boat grew lighter, swimming like a leaf." Sixteen splashes are completed...where is the last one? The men delay, preparing a noose around Phrosyni's neck, tying her to a rock to make sure the corpse will go down. A heavy noise comes, a splash with foam, ripples that "Like large wreaths reach Ali's feet before they die."

The poet ends the narrative with a wish and a curse. Those ripples will one day become mighty waves that will encircle Ali in his prison island, in the very same lake:

> Rising like mountains, they will block
> Your way ... cruel, thirsting for revenge.

III *Critique of* Kyra Phrosyni

Though popular in its time, *Kyra Phrosyni* is one of the few major poems in modern Greek literature that suffers from almost total critical neglect, a neglect that has substantially contributed to the decline of Valaoritis' reputation and to the general ignorance about his work. Even friendly critics have had little to say about this poem, usually dismissing it as too romantic, or sentimental. Only a few have written more than a passing remark, notably Paul Nirvanas, and especially Kostis Palamas, who made some brief but illuminating comments on the poem.

Some early critics praised *Kyra Phrosyni* for patriotic rather than for aesthetic reasons. Dimitrios Vikelas, for instance, writing one year after the publication of the poem, greeted Valaoritis as the author of "new poetry" that was destined to arouse the Greeks to fight a new war for the liberation of Epirus. *Kyra Phrosyni* circulated widely both at home and abroad, and won Valaoritis praise in the foreign press.[13] Laskaratos, who was laboring hard to find subscribers for his newspaper *Lychnos* at that time, asked Valaoritis' permission to reprint portions of the poem, which Valaoritis granted gladly.[14] *Kyra Phrosyni*, in fact, continued to be popular until the death of Valaoritis, in 1879, when Roidis published an article in the periodical *Estia*, reassessing, among other things, many of the current views about Valaoritis' poetry. Roidis criticized Valaoritis for lack of control over his material, but liked the vivid descriptions of the Lake of Jannina and the scenes of horror at Ali's court, comparing them for power and inspiration to scenes in Dante's *The Inferno*.[15]

Of the more recent critics, Angelos Sikelianos, a warm supporter of Valaoritis as a poet and man, regards all his early poetry as suffering from excesses of rhetoric, with "contrasts imperfectly transformed."[16] Aristos Kambanis, editor of two popular volumes of Valaoritis' poetry, calls *Phrosyni* "a series of sentimental paroxysms."[17] In his *History of Modern Greek Literature*, K. Th. Dimaras finds *Kyra Phrosyni*, as well as *Athanasis Diakos*, exhibiting the defects of romanticism—particularly excesses in the drawing of characters and the dramatization of myth.[18] But the poem also had its admirers: Paul Nirvanas, speaking to the literary club "Parnassus" in 1916, finds *Kyra Phrosyni* "a unique discovery as a theme for a romantic poem." Its subject is drawn directly from the tradition of the folk songs, many of which had paved the way for the composition of an epic poem of large dimensions. Phrosyni, the protagonist, is, according to Nirvanas, "a unique figure among the gallery of tragic women." Living under the shadow of Ali, in an atmosphere of passions and intrigue, "she refused to exchange the son's youth for the blood-dripping age of the father." The revenge that follows her rejection of the tyrant's love would have been an unusual episode "even in the pages of Roman history." This revenge is unique "not only for its tragic quality but also for the grandeur of its staging—as it was conceived and executed by the scorned love and wounded admiration of this oriental Caligula."[19]

Palamas, the only Greek critic to examine the work of Valaoritis with some care, approves of Valaoritis' "sublime scheme" to create poetry that would serve the national ideals and needs of the Greek nation. But he claims in an early article that

Phrosyni "unfortunately is not brought together by that indissoluble bond between form and content, and, as a result, the reader has no clear perception of each of these elements."[20] Later, Palamas developed some appreciation for this poem; though he still found weaknesses in structure and characterization, he felt that the heroine exhibits breadth of conception and symbolizes the Greek soul.

Like the national soul, fallen, sinful, she does not begin to have a clear understanding of her lofty destiny until she is enslaved. After the humiliation—oppressed, suffering, and tortured, like the Greek soul—Phrosyni fights to free herself from the bondage of the infamous Pasha. Then, suddenly, she is illumined by a divine light, and she becomes transformed from a romantic lovelorn damsel to a mystical heroine.[21]

But viewed as a work of art, Palamas observes, *Kyra Phrosyni* suffers. The poem is melodramatic, verbose, and awkward in its descriptions. It is fraught with psychological inconsistencies: the heroine, for instance, changes too abruptly from a sinner into a martyr with no plausibility or preparation. The verses are too loose and artless, and the demotic idiom is used hesitatingly, with no authority. As a composition, the poem fails, but as an idea it is conceived within the grand design of the national epic characteristic of Valaoritis' poetry and plays a definite role in it. Besides, the poem offers a fascinating portrait of the villain Ali, who is drawn within the framework of the Hugoan contrasts of light and darkness, piety and satanism, deeply flawed conscience with sharp pangs of remorse, a monstrous ego with mock humility. There are also good sections in *Phrosyni*, especially those which describe the Greek manliness (*levendiá*) of the warriors. In fact, Palamas claims, the poet has done nothing more than perform a perpetual memorial service in honor of those who died for the cause of freedom before and during the Greek War of Independence.

IV *Introduction to* Athanasis Diakos

Valaoritis composed *Athanasis Diakos* between 1864 and 1866, a period marked by the first major disappointments of his political career. As national politics had begun to disillusion him, he sought refuge in the quiet of his villa at Madouri, where he spent more and more time. During the summer of 1865, he worked incessantly on the poem, "refusing to have anything to do with politics."[22] The poem was finished in 1866 after hard work from January through March, but the preface and notes took him the rest of the year to complete, as the outbreak of the Cretan Revolution kept him busy travelling back and forth to Athens. *Athanasis Diakos,* with "Astrapoyiannos," a shorter poem, came out in Athens in the spring of 1867 while the political career of Valaoritis was reaching its peak.[23]

This poem's purpose and scope are best understood against the background of the political events which helped shape the life of its author at that time. Valaoritis' brief sojourn in the political arena of Athens had already convinced him that he could rely neither on the rapidly alternating Greek governments, nor on the will of the national assembly to carry out the struggle for the liberation of the rest of Greece's lands. The Union of the Ionian islands with Greece, a goal to which he had personally contributed, had fanned his hopes of further national accomplishments. He envisaged a unified nation that would go to any lengths of self-sacrifice to obtain its goals. But in Athens he found that most politicians were driven by selfish aims and personal ambition, while the parties wasted their energies in a contest to grab power. Fleeing from this ugly reality, he spent as much time as he could at Madouri, where "he lived in a constant dream, in the company of the old-time klephts," as Roidis puts it.[24]

The poem, then, must be understood as a reaction to this bleak political reality, and at the same time as a means of providing a contrast between the glorious past and the ignominious present. In the past, the poet tells us in the Preface, the Greek nation "had one dream, one dogma, one divine, noble, and great purpose—which was pursued unceasingly with complete disregard for imprisonment, torture, even execution."[25] "What a difference," Valaoritis exclaims, "exists between those actions of heroism and the present apathy, deadness of spirit, and pettiness of our men!"[26] He felt that the warlike spirit of the race had been extinguished, and the arms of the forefathers were rusting away while "the descendants of the armatoloi had turned into petty lawyers, eternally wrangling and pecking at one another."[27] The poet wanted to present the revolutionary hero, Diakos, as the supreme example of the armatoloi, capable of providing an archetype of manliness and inspiration to the Greeks of his generation.

That the poem must be seen in the context of political action is also attested by Valaoritis' son and biographer, John Valaoritis:

It is a coincidence, but certainly a very strange one, that *Diakos* was written on the eve of a patriotic uprising, and was printed at a time when the revolution in Crete was in full swing. During this period Valaoritis, as a deputy and as a citizen, inside and outside the assembly, was hard at work supporting his fighting brothers. One may recall here that both the *Mnemosyna* and *Phrosyni* were produced under similar circumstances. One would think that his heart beat in harmony with the heartbeats of the nation.[28]

In the Preface to *Diakos*, Valaoritis makes claims similar to those made in *Kyra Phrosyni* regarding the role of history in the writing of national poetry.[29] But in this poem he shifts the locale of action from Epirus to Alamana, from a northwestern extremity to central Greece, where most of the fighting of the Greek War of Independence took place. For the first time in his poetry he also makes a chronological shift, from the pre-revolutionary period to the time of the war itself. It seems that whatever he wrote before the composition of *Diakos* was a preamble, a preparatory course of action describing the main events leading to the revolution. Valaoritis wrote with a large plan in mind, and what he wanted to produce finally was a larger canvas depicting the entire scene of the war. His poetry, according to Palamas, taken as a whole, reveals in its broad outlines the epic cycle of the national struggle for existence and identity. The individual poems are pieces of a whole.[30] The writing of *Diakos* clearly shows the progress toward this goal.

The episode that furnishes the action of the poem is the Battle of Alamana, on April 14, 1822,[31] during which Diakos

and a few companions attempted to block the passage of the
Turkish and Albanian forces marching southward toward Pelo-
ponnesos. As Valaoritis explains in the Preface, he studied the
available historical material in great detail,[32] confident that his
painstaking efforts to render facts accurately would demonstrate
his point that poetry could have a historical basis. It was, however, the actual person of Diakos that attracted him most. Above
all other Greek warriors, it seemed to him that Diakos possessed
qualities that were especially representative of Greek excellence.
In the Preface Diakos is described as "the hero, a God-fearing
athlete, the model of physical and spiritual beauty, the true
and genuine offspring of medieval Greek manhood, the un-
assuming fighter, the apostle."[33]

Diakos' early training in the church accounted for his strong
religious beliefs and for his chastity. His family name was
Grammatikos, which was changed to Diakos, a derivation of
diakonos, meaning "deacon." He left the monastery at an early
age because his striking beauty aroused the passion of a lewd
Turkish aga from Dorkis, who invited Diakos to come and work
at his service. Diakos at once escaped to the mountains where
he joined the band of the then famous chieftain, Dimos Skaltsas.
In no time, Diakos became known throughout Greece for his
prudence, fearlessness, integrity of character, and for his physical
abilities in running, marksmanship, and the long jump. He
won the confidence of his fellow warriors and soon rose in rank
to hold an important post as *armatolos* of Leivadiá—a place not
far from the ancient Thermopylae. Later, Diakos joined the
forces of Ali Pasha at Jannina, training there in a military camp
with other Greek warriors whom Ali had managed to attract
around him. But Diakos left Ali's corrupt environment when
he discovered that Ali had plans to assassinate him. In 1818
he joined the *Philiki Etaireia,* an organization throughout the
Balkans aiming at the liberation of Greece, and was reappointed
armatolos of Leivadiá. When the revolution began, he was a
powerful leader with several hundred select men in his command.
During the operations of 1822, along with several other chieftains, he was assigned to defend the narrow passage near
Thermopylae against a vast Turkish army headed by Kioshe
Mehmet Pasha and Omer Vrioni, who descended from the north

under orders to crush the Greek rebellion. Most of the other
chieftains scattered, but Diakos, against the advice of his friends,
stayed at this post and fought to the last. Wounded, he was
arrested and brought before Omer Vrioni, who offered to pardon
him if he would join his forces. Diakos rejected the offer
and was subsequently impaled and burned alive.

With the writing of *Diakos*, Valaoritis had another aim in
mind—namely, to promote his favorite theory that the demotic
language was sufficiently rich to cover all the needs of modern
Greek poetry. He wrote his wife, expressing his determination
to render the demotic in its "rustic grace" and in "all its classic
beauty."[34] *Diakos*, he tells us in his Preface, must remain free
of all foreign elements, especially of romantic plots which
are imitations of western customs and traditions. "Native literature," he claims, "must remain free of such influences, which
contaminate and corrupt the true character of native Greek
letters."[35] To preserve the purity of the poem in this sense,
Valaoritis even kept it free from classical names—something
that no other modern Greek author has managed to do. Even
the most glorious of these, he explains, would conflict with the
tone and harmony of the poem. Though the action of *Diakos*
takes place near antiquity's most famous battlefield, no mention
is made of Leonidas or Thermopylae. "But the names of Greece's
oppressors," Valaoritis notes, "fit completely and merge into the
texture of folk poetry, either because of time and the proximity
of races, or because contrasts and antagonisms conceal im-
perceptible and invisible points of contact, which contribute to
the formation of works of art."[36]

V *A Plot Summary of* Athanasis Diakos

Athanasis Diakos, a relatively short poem for its subject, runs
into a compact 1,230 lines, nearly half the length of *Kyra
Phrosyni*; it is subdivided into six cantos, of which the first,
second, and last average less than 110 lines each. The most
substantial are the third, with 413 lines, and the fourth and
fifth, with approximately 250 lines each. The action moves rapidly
and is rarely interrupted by lengthy speeches (with the exception
of the prayer of Diakos in the first canto) or other interjections

and digressions such as those that characterized *Phrosyni*. The
entire poem centers on one episode—the battle, arrest, and
martyrdom of Diakos. The work was composed with meticulous
care, and in structure, unity of theme and action, and unity of
tone it is without doubt the most successful of Valaoritis' poems.

Canto I. "The Eve of Battle." The first canto begins with
Diakos' sharply phrased command to his lieutenant, Mitros, to
climb the mountaintop to scout the approaching Turkish forces.
As the loyal Mitros obeys instantly, "vanishing like a shooting
star," Diakos invites his companions around him, and asks them
to pray together with him. Night is falling. The craggy peaks,
the ravines, the trees, fountains, wild flowers, the sky, the wind
silently listen to the prayer. Though somewhat lengthy and
diffuse, this passage is meant to demonstrate the piety of Diakos
and the simplicity of his faith. He had always prayed to his
Heavenly Father not to let him be killed in battle until he
had a chance to fight for his country's liberty. His wish is now
granted; he is ready to fight and die.

When the prayer is done, he kisses the earth, and sheds a
tear which falls on the grass—"Lucky grass that drank from such
a fountain!" the poet interjects. Nature now keeps vigil for
him; spring embraces him, the flowers kiss his forehead. Even
the lowly weeds creep around him as he rests among them,
mixing into his hair, desiring to acquire immortal fame. As the
lion-hearted Diakos falls asleep, silence falls around him; sleep
becomes "a parapet, arresting time in its destructive march."
These and other elaborate metaphors end the canto: Diakos'
tear will wash the blemishes that the nation has suffered throughout the dark, long night of its slavery; Diakos is like an eagle
in its nest, "hatching" a whole new nation.

Canto II. "The Three Men." When the second canto opens,
Diakos is still asleep. As dawn cracks, two chieftains, Diovouniotis and Panourias, arrive from their nearby posts to confer
with Diakos about the impending battle. Both men stop for a
moment to marvel at the serene innocence of Diakos, who is
still sleeping peacefully. They are impressed by the radiance,
the "clarity" of his face and forehead, wondering how he can

sleep without fear or anxiety. Diakos wakes and begs their pardon for having obliged them to wait. He explains that his heart is not made of stone and that his deep sleep had been caused by an omen, a falling star—his fate compassionately allowing him to become used to death. He asks them to take care of the living; he will have to fight to protect the honor of the dead forefathers of the nation, throwing himself into the flames of the battle, "incense to the terrible sacrifice."

One of the men advises Diakos not to waste himself. The nation has only a few drops of blood left, and these must be spared. But Diakos rejects the advice; he cannot yield, he says, he cannot go away; the fight for freedom demands this sacrifice. Besides, Omer Pasha Vrioni had better find a few dozen bodies to stumble upon before crossing the mountain pass. If need be, Diakos will stay and fight all alone. His hands and feet will sprout roots into the ground, and the enemy will have to cut him to pieces to remove him. Dazzled by the hero's eyes and face, Panourias thinks for a moment that Diakos has grown tall and great like Olympus. Diakos reprimands the old warrior for his doubts about the outcome of the battle, then asks him to go and tell the other chieftains that the struggle for liberty has begun with the church holding the banner; others must imitate her and support her. The two elder chieftains promise to do so. In the meantime, Mitros returns, bringing news that Omer Vrioni is near. The battle is about to begin.

Canto III. "Twenty-Third of April." This canto begins with a euphoric scene in which the poet describes the beauty of an April morning. The partridge sings as the sun shines through the ravine. The hawk "Flies like a shot to Heaven . . . ," while far away on the mountains the snow melts, falling from rock to rock. The wheat ripening in the fields glances now and then at the young warrior, who reflects for a moment on the beauty of the life he must lose. Silence prevails; in the midst of nature, teeming with life, no human voice is heard, no shepherd's pipe, no ploughman's cry.

The three hundred warriors are resting, sitting or sprawling on the ground, silently awaiting the hour of the battle. The banner of Diakos, carrying the image of St. George, is waving

above their heads. As they gradually shake off sleep and begin
their battle preparations, a thin mist comes up from the ravine,
like a shadow bringing the ghosts of the dead to Diakos. Among
the bushes the "iron mare" can be seen waiting, ready for war,
"Sterile, a winged snake, grazing in the cool...." Diakos had
brought her from Jannina, and named her "Astero." In the
background one can hear the hollow roar of the approaching
army—like the roar of the ocean.

One of the men asks Diamantis, an old warrior, to tell them
about his past life. In a passage noted for its realism, the old
man describes his long years in the service of his country,
fighting oppression:

> Forty years I have fought. Blades, bullets
> Have torn my skin from head to toe ...
> I've walked about naked, hungry,
> My bleeding heels dyeing the thorns,
> Hail has battered me. I've made my bed
> Inside a wolf's den. Hunted like a beast,
> I've searched the ground for acorns to eat.
> Often, I had to bite a lead bullet to quench
> my thirst. . . .

Cheers come from the other warriors as they hear his tale.
Then they ask him to interpret for them the blade bone of a
lamb they had just eaten, gift of a friendly bishop from Antonina.
The old man, who is also a makeshift diviner, reads the bone
with apprehension; his eyes follow a forked vein.. .black
cypresses scattered around, clearing, a dark spot, a wedge. The
old man pauses suddenly—a black line, serpentlike, appears at
the side of the bone. He seems dismayed, and the men
ask him to explain what he has seen. He invites them to observe
what appears to be a double head emerging from a cloud with
wide-stretched wings. The bird holds a sword on one wing,
a cross on the other. Dazzling sunrays surround it. The men
stand around Diamantis, looking incredulously at the marvelous
image. But before he has time to answer their questions, a
sudden noise is heard, a neighing from the mare. "It's Mitros!
He's back!" someone exclaims.

Mitros approaches, bleeding. A bullet grazed him as he hurried to bring back the news—bad news: Omer Pasha attacked Diovouniotis, the chieftain protecting the gorge, who then fled without firing a shot! Some of the other chieftains put up determined resistance for a while, but the Albanian troops were too numerous. Most of the Greeks were slaughtered; others fled. One chieftain, Kalyvas, Mitros reports, was still holding fast at Alamana. Kioshe Mehmet, the other Turkish general, is descending on Diakos' post from another direction.

Athanasis now gives last instructions to his men: they must shoot straight; every one of their bullets must count for an enemy dead. If he is killed, they must make sure his weapons and his head do not fall into the enemy's hands. His talisman, a medallion around his neck, must be given to St. John's monastery. His ring, however, must not be removed from his finger, in order that Omer Pasha should recognize him. The ring bears the stamp of faith—a cross, and a double-headed bird. Diakos speaks allegorically:

> Rains have come, we must sow today,
> The earth was fallow, we must plant it;
> The harvest will come....

Then he appoints the men to their posts. They prepare for battle, their eyes shining like coals from behind the bushes. Diakos feels joy in his strength, but for a moment a cloud passes over his broad, sun-illumined forehead. A bitterness burns him as if he had drunk hemlock; he now understands that he will die. What is he to say to the dead warriors when he meets them in the other world? Has he been worthy of them? But these thoughts are dispersed as the battle begins.

Omer Vrioni is marching at the head of his Albanian troops, leading the attack, while Kioshe Mehmet is making a circle around the troops of Kalyvas. The description becomes graphic, terse: one man falls, troops cross the bridge below Diakos and his men, smoke covers everything. The chieftains at Alamana, Kalyvas and Vlachoyiannis, are under great pressure; their troops are about to scatter. Diakos orders sixty of his best men to go to their aid.

A dervish appears marching ahead of the Turkish troops, holding the severed heads of two Greek warriors. Diakos' men look at him in horror. To intimidate the Greeks, the dervish throws the heads on the ground and tramples on them. A messenger suddenly stands on a rock, trying to attract the Greeks' attention. They ask him what he wants. "Let us pass through and our master, Omer Pasha, will grant your every wish," he cries. "Tell him that we have no master," the Greeks shout back. The traitor tries in vain to cajole the rebels, telling them that he too is a Greek, one who has come to his senses. The klephts curse the traitor loudly, and their curse reverberates through the ravine, "poisoning the air." The Albanians push on, flooding the place like ants on a hill. Vrioni urges his troops on, prodding them as though they were yoked oxen. Diakos gives the order to fire: all the pain, hatred, revenge of the defenders are released at once. "Fire! Brothers, fire!"

> The bullet of Athanasis does not want human
> flesh; it goes straight for the horse, razes
> the throat. The stallion stands straight in
> a last, proud leap, its gums bleeding, its
> joints loosening; then tumbles on the ground.
> In its death beat, it still keeps its ears erect.

The dervish who carries the two heads is next. Another terse description follows:

> The old rifle roared. The dervish croaked and
> fell back kicking, his hands still planted in the
> hair of the two heads.... "Did I miss, Mitros?"
> Diamantis said. "You broke his skull, right between
> the seams, you gave him a third eye, so he can now
> find his way through Hell...."

Around the dervish's body many young men die, resembling buds swept down by the torrent.

Greeks and Albanians fall. But the troops of Vrioni are countless, and fresh ones keep arriving to replace those who are killed. Bullets fly like hailstones; blood drenches the earth, making brothers of the dying men. Diamantis implores Diakos to leave, but Diakos rejects the advice. He calls the remaining men around him, only ten now, and together they rush toward the nearby monastery, their last defense. They leap over the fences, raising dust, startling the vultures nesting on the surrounding trees. The deserted chapel echoes with the shots, the walls are soon bespattered with blood, the bells in the belfry toll as they are hit by flying bullets.

With all his companions fallen, Athanasis is still fighting alone. But his pistols are empty and his blade is broken to the scabbard. The enemy fall on him and seize him alive, wounded as he is, putting him in chains. The battle is still raging nearby at the inn of Alamana, which is holding. With a joyous shout, Diakos greets his fellow fighters as he passes. But those valiant men are soon silenced, as darkness falls over the gorge and the sun sets behind the mountains. The birds hide in their nests on the battlefield. Only the wolves are heard giving an occasional grunt as they dismember the dead bodies of the warriors.

Canto IV. "The Revolution." The fourth canto begins with a transition in locale—the camp of the enemy. The Albanian soldiers are asleep, smeared with blood and exhausted from the labors of the battle. The dawn is still deep, the moon has not yet set. The moonlight lingers heavily upon the trees and the meadows. The earth seems empty and deserted, like the sea. A hollow oak tree haunts the place. Poisonous weeds, described with stark realism, grow around it. Ghostlike, the tree appears to have grown gigantic, as if trying to reach heaven. The scene has allegorical significance. The oak symbolizes the Turkish Empire—immense, trying with its presumptuous height to reach heaven, but evil and hollow inside. A gypsy is lodged in the hollow with his instruments of torture. He is old, in rags, consumptive, pock-marked. He is a symbol of ugliness and evil, envious of the good and beautiful in nature, hating what is youthful and healthy. He harbors a special hatred for stars, flowers, children. He is a pocket of evil in the universe. He is the one who will soon torture Diakos, who lies chained at the root of the tree.

The gypsy's torture implements and his sadistic treatment

of Diakos are described vividly in a scene of "Gothic" horror. Diakos suffers, but he is not alone: God is present, and the souls of the great dead of the past, the fighters who died in the struggle for freedom, visit him. In a long descriptive scene, Diakos descends, as in a dream, to the underworld, as all epic heroes must do in the course of their adventures. The most famous chieftains and warriors of the prerevolutionary period and those who have died during the war appear to him in a vision and attempt to impart to him their courage and strength of heart. At once, the tree seems to come alive, transformed into the Bishop Isaiah, who takes Diakos through the air, arriving at a high spot from where they can view Constantinople and the last Byzantine emperor—a symbol of the fall of the empire, but also of the hopes of the rising new nation. The bishop announces to Diakos the resurrection of the nation; the long line of dead martyrs will build a bridge toward freedom with their bones. In a series of vivid pictures, Diakos sees the hanging of Patriarch Gregorios, the dragging of the body through the streets by a mob, and the casting of the holy relic into the sea of Bosporus. The corpse later rises to the surface and "sails" on the top of the waves. The dead patriarch floats away, toward the abyss; his martyrdom, the poet tells us, will awaken the conscience of the nation. "Shall we not reach the other shore, too?" asks Diakos. "Will the dead not see this land once?" "Have faith, Diakos," the bishop replies. Dawn breaks as Diakos awakes, drawing away from the magnificent vision. He sees the gypsy, the leaves of the oak tree, its hellish branches, a horrible reality.

Canto V. "Omer Vrioni." The fifth canto deals with the meeting of the captive Diakos and the Albanian, Omer Pasha Vrioni. We are told in vivid detail the story of Vrioni's career in the service of the sultan, his wars in the Orient, his victories, his days in the camp of Ali Pasha. With all his successes, Vrioni has not found fulfillment in the life of a hired fighter; he is restless, his conscience darkened with remorse. He is, of course, presented in such a way as to provide a contrast to Diakos, who is seen in the dazzling light of superb valor and clear conscience. Vrioni feels guilty, for he is intelligent and under-

stands the nature of the crime he is about to commit. Diakos
is in pain, but the knowledge of the meaning of his sacrifice
gives him strength to endure his fate. Vrioni is envious of
Diakos' virtue and moral character; he remembers quite well
how much he liked the proud Greek warriors when they were
practicing the arts of war in Ali's camp many years ago.

Diakos is brought before Vrioni in chains. Seemingly interested in the captive, Vrioni asks him details about his arrest.
How is it that a man like him was taken alive? Diakos replies
that he was saving the last bullet for himself but was compelled
to use it to kill the traitor who asked him to surrender.

> "If I fell into your hands, what would you
>   do with me, Diakos?"
> "I'd give you back your arms and let you
>   fight me."

Vrioni does not like this answer; it is too proud. But he attempts
to cajole Diakos into submission, reminding him of his friendli-
ness to the Greeks and the sympathy he always showed for
their cause. Wasn't it he who, ordered once by Ali to murder
Greek chieftains, gave them a warning instead and helped them
escape? Doesn't Athanasis know that he and Vrioni come from
the same ancestors, that the "seed" of Christianity is in him?
The two of them could become brothers again, rightfully so,
and united they could fight and defeat the sultan. "I will keep
Albania, the rest is yours," he finally declares. Diakos tells him
that if he means this, he must give proof of his sincerity; he
must kiss the two-headed eagle and cross on Diakos' ring which
Vrioni is now wearing. Vrioni declines to answer, and abruptly
asks for a yes or no from Diakos. "No! I will not give a handful
of earth, not a drop of water to an infidel."

A clatter of horse hooves is heard from outside, and a guard
rushes in to announce the arrival of Kioshe Mehmet. Looking
uneasy, Vrioni begs Diakos not to reveal what transpired between
them. Diakos assures him that he will keep the secret; Vrioni
appreciates this and asks Diakos if he wants something in return.
Diakos says, "Yes, give the ring to me." Vrioni worries that this
will reveal the trade between them. Diakos points to his mouth;

Vrioni understands and gives the ring to him; Diakos kisses
it and swallows it.

Kioshe Mehmet enters, and a "dark, muddy flood follows his
steps, like a wave that sweeps away weeds on the beach...."
Mehmet chides Vrioni for his lack of enthusiasm in dealing
with the prisoner. Orientals (as distinguished from Albanians,
who were a conquered people) have only one purpose, and
that is "to widen the wasteland, to enlarge the tomb of the
Greeks." He must kill and burn, in order to stay alive. "For five
hundred years," he explains, "these flintstones of Greece have
obtained what soil they have from our dead bodies." No Muslem
can go to sleep without dreaming of "whistling swords or the
flash of a gun." Kioshe has lost his patience; this time he means
business. He will turn this land upside down, dig it, disembowel
it, to see what devils inhabit it. Halil Bei, one of his hangmen,
observes that the klephts must be wiped out once and for all.
"Uproot them from the soil, to make sure they will never
sprout again!" he shouts.

Diakos is asked once more to submit and worship the Prophet.
Once more he defies his captors. "Our skin is too tough to
burn!" he says when he is informed that he will be roasted alive.

Canto VI. "The Ring." The sixth canto begins with a lyrical
description of the beauty of day. As the end nears, Diakos finds
it unbearable that he must die in the prime of life, when the
spring is blossoming and the hawks fly free. This is the classic
complaint, uttered by all young heroes who have to die for
a noble cause. This scene is rendered in spare poetic strokes; a
few poignant lines ending with a. famous distich from a
demotic song:

> See what time Charon chose to take me,
> Now that the earth is green and the trees have flower

Diakos is now driven to the place of execution. On the way,
he is insulted and humiliated beyond human endurance. He
is trampled under horse hooves, stepped upon, bitten in the
face by the bravos' horses. It is hot and humid, the smoldering
air carries threats and mocking laughter. The sky is empty,

no swallow's song is heard to refresh his spirit. The road seems
endless. Like walls, the rows of sullen Albanian soldiers enclose
him on either side. Diakos calls out to them, asking for someone
to take pity on him and shoot him. Isn't there an "honest
Albanian" among them? The soldiers look at one another mutely
for a moment, seemingly unmoved. But a tiny noise is heard,
as if a finger raised a pistol's hammer. Halil Bei shouts, "Dog,
put your arms down, whoever you are. This one's mine, my
gift. . . ." And like a bat, he clings to Diakos' hair. The soldiers
at once jump on the captive, shouting, leaping in the air, and
tossing curses at him. They drag him toward the holm oak,
where the gypsy is readying his instruments; two forks on the
ground to support the spit. Diakos is tied and impaled. The
fire is made of green branches so that it will last; it now crackles,
ready; the tree above witnesses the sight. Diakos offers a last
prayer:

> Christ, make these ashes a cool dew
> To fall on the earth and sprout new riches. . . .

Then he surrenders his spirit. His naked flesh is gradually hidden
behind thick smoke. The gypsy turns the spit quickly, like a
spinning wheel. Halil Bei shouts at him to slow down, the fire
is consuming the body too fast. But the smoke becomes thicker,
gigantic, concealing the relic. Frightened, the gypsy runs away
from the conflagration. The holm oak catches fire and burns
down—the body of Diakos is swallowed up in the blaze.

The fire finally subsides. The executioners draw near the
scene, but they can see nothing, the holy corpse had vanished.
They dig the ashes trying to find a bone, to discover a sign.
Nothing! Only some sparks and a bright ring of smoke ascend
toward heaven. "When, Athanasis, when, shall we find your
ring and wear it again?" asks the poet.

Tamed now, the monsters depart growling. The gypsy withdraws and settles once again in his hole. The site is deserted
except for the rays of the sun kissing the holy remains.

VI   *A Critique of* Athanasis Diakos

The first major poem of Valaoritis to be published in Athens,
Athanasis Diakos was largely ignored by critics, and has not

been such a favorite with the Greek public as other poems of
Valaoritis have. *Diakos* never had the popular success of the
Mnemosyna and *Kyra Phrosyni*, or of some of the shorter
poems. Valaoritis was not immensely popular as a poet in Athens,
though he was highly esteemed as a statesman and parliamentary
orator. The Athenian literati, especially the representatives of
the Romantic School, still using the *katharevousa* in composing
their poetry, had difficulty with Valaoritis' folk idiom and showed
little enthusiasm for his literary aims as stated in the preface
of his poem. The periodical *National Library*, edited by Dimitrios
Paparrigopoulos, published a page of adverse criticism,[37] while
a major poet[38] declared that with *Diakos* Valaoritis' decline had
begun. Even Roidis, in a piece of major criticism written in
the year of the poet's death, made only a passing reference to
Diakos, while devoting paragraphs on *Kyra Phrosyni* and other
poems. *Diakos* had to wait until 1889, when Palamas published
his first article on Valaoritis, to receive notice proportional
to its merit.

Palamas, by far the most perceptive critic of the work of
Valaoritis, not only accepts the thesis that Greece's national
poetry must be based on its recent history, but also finds that
Diakos fits the definition in almost every respect. *Diakos*, he
claims, possesses all the ingredients of the national epic—form
and content harmoniously interrelated, and unity of language
and subject matter. Answering the charge of Roidis that a
modern Greek epic would be an anachronism, Palamas states
that, on the contrary, heroic poetry is quite proper, since myths
and traditions still have value in Greek culture. Furthermore,
he claims, the epic should be revived in the country where it
was born. The new nation has its heroic period just behind it;
the revolution produced the popular songs that are the background and foundation of all epic poetry. The time is ripe, he
writes, for this generation of poets to sing the feats of national
heroes, fitting the fragments together and constructing the epic
of modern Greece.

In the same article, Palamas also offers sustained, close
analysis of the prosody and versification of the poem, showing
how Valaoritis borrowed from the technique of the popular
songs and how he departed from them. In *Diakos* Valaoritis used

the fifteen syllable line in iambic meter, ending in an unrhymed
unaccented syllable—a device that helps to create dramatic
suspense and tension. Accents, Palamas continues, "descend with
force and clatter, like hail; the rhythm gasps and stops and
again rises mightily as a giant fighting a furious battle."[39]
Valaoritis did not merely imitate the fifteen syllable line from
the folk songs; he amplified and enriched it, giving it variety.
The rhythm in the popular songs, while forceful and very
expressive, is at the same time monotonous, depending on
frequent repetition of sentence patterns which finally tire the
reader. In contrast, Valaoritis' rhythm is more complex and
consistent with the demands of conscious poetic art. His language achieves perfection; it is "rich, abundant, self-sufficient,
drawing from its own resources all its charms and beauties."[40]
The poet was not satisfied with the use of the demotic and
the knowledge derived from the study of folk songs. He took
pains to come in touch with the common people, "as if a pure
rhapsodist of ancient times; he ran through the mountains,
he spent nights in the hut of the farmer; thus he enriched
his poetry and at the same time filled the treasury of the
Greek language."[41] In his poetry Valaoritis never sought the
help of *katharevousa*, and never used classical names "for
fear that these would spoil the austere symphony of the wholly
warlike verses." He avoided this mixture "from a sense of highly
aesthetic principles."[42]

In a later article,[43] Palamas makes further comments on
Diakos, praising it as a conscious improvement over *Kyra
Phrosyni*. Diakos is a Leonidas, planting himself before the
hordes of barbarians descending on Greece. The poet presents
the character of his hero with Homeric objectivity, describing
the Turks and Albanians with impartiality, as Homer does the
Trojans. But the art of Valaoritis is more dramatic than epic;
the poet does not narrate, he presents action on a stage.
Valaoritis lacks the detachment of Homer, who stands above
the events he narrates with cosmic calm. The poet of *Diakos*
lives the action he describes, fighting with his hero rather
than singing his glory. Though he does not appear in the action,
never using the first person, his presence is felt. One can almost
see him fighting in the battle, striking, being struck, running,

shouting war cries, bleeding, falling. The rhythm of the verses
follows closely the rapid course of action, leaving the reader
breathless. The supernatural element, on the other hand, adds
mystery. *Diakos* remains a poem, not a chapter in Greek history.
But the miracles—the "revelation" in the fourth canto, and the
ascension of the ring in the last—are described sparsely, dis-
playing a "Greek restraint" in Valaoritis, a sense of form. The
supernatural is presented with naturalness, as in Homer and
Aeschylus.

But for all its sweeping power, *Diakos* is not entirely free of
defects. The reader cannot rid himself of an impression of
discomfort created by the poem's monotony. The atmosphere
in *Diakos* is stifling; there is a harsh, rigid, almost fanatical
domination of the masculine element. In his efforts to avoid
a "romantic plot," Valaoritis kept his poem free of any features
that could produce feelings of softness and passivity; no relief
adorns its lines, no interruption of the severe atmosphere of
battle and martyrdom is allowed. Nothing interferes with the
purity of the historical theme.

Palamas' criticism on *Diakos* remains to this day the most
substantial in Greek letters. Other critics have offered only
sporadic comments, generally dismissing *Diakos* as a poem that
exemplifies the defects, rather than the virtues, of the poetry
of Valaoritis. Paul Nirvanas complains that the subject matter
of the poem is too meager for a composition of large breadth.
Five whole cantos are devoted to the description of one
episode, leaving gaps to be filled with abundant rhetoric—
orations, dialogues, visions, elements "not organic to the epic
character of the poem."[44] Dimaras finds *Diakos* a romantic
poem, especially in the development of the familiar Byronic
contrasts and the drawing of characters.[45] Sikelianos groups
Diakos with *Phrosyni*, calling these two poems "lively and
admirable stages" in the poetic development of Valaoritis, but
still deeply affected by romantic tendencies of exaggeration
and antitheses.[46] Some critics have high praise for *Diakos*:
Aristos Kambanis calls it Valaoritis' most complete poem, "a
truly poetic achievement." "The unrhymed fifteen syllable line
(*politikos stichos*)," Kambanis continues, "does not have the
monotony of the folk song; it has sinews...With its variety

and tightness of construction, it fully serves the needs of epic narration."[47]

Another admirer, Spiros Melas, claims that *Diakos* is Valaoritis' masterpiece, "a kind of epic work, distinctly and completely Greek." In this poem, "language, rhythm, shaping power, dramatic energy, imagery, richness of imagination, all have attained a high level of perfection, contributing to a vigorous and harmonious whole."[48] Even Nirvanas, after having done with his adverse criticism, states: "With all its defects, *Diakos* shows the heroic poet in his most characteristic and poetic note."[49]

CHAPTER 5

Poems: 1857–1879

BETWEEN 1857 and 1879 Valaoritis wrote numerous short poems, some of which were published in local papers and magazines, while most of them remained in manuscript form and were collected by his son, John, in the Maraslis edition of 1908. Some were sent in lieu of condolence letters on the occasion of the death of friends and relatives. Some of the most famous—like "The Rock and the Wave" and "To Patriarch Gregorios V"—were composed to be recited in public or read at social gatherings.

About fifty in number, these poems show Valaoritis in a variety of moods, expressing emotions and ideas other than those described in his earlier poetry. To be sure, he seems to be carrying on the same heroic purpose found in the *Mnemosyna* poems, praising the exploits of heroes, or attempting to establish the contrast between the glorious past and the lethargic present. But as he grew older, and especially after his retirement from politics in 1869, Valaoritis ventured into themes and concerns other than those of the strictly patriotic kind. Many of the poems of this period show a man of greater emotional depth than his early poems had revealed, a man who had grown wiser, more detached, and philosophical with the vicissitudes of life. The theme of death, in particular, many be said to be the only theme to have drawn Valaoritis into philosophical speculation. Pained over the loss of three young daughters and of other young people in his area, Valaoritis continued to brood over the subject of death, a subject that had preoccupied him since his earliest days. But death was no longer seen as a means of catharsis and regeneration, as when Katsandonis, Samuel, Diakos, Phrosyni, and other heroes had died. Their deaths were necessary sacrifices and examples of heroism in the process of the fight

114

for freedom. The deaths of young innocent people around him, on the other hand, were to him gratuitous and hard to explain facts, forcing him into a mood of introspection and self-analysis. Propelled by his anguish, he asked, "Why should the young die?" Like Dostoyevsky, Valaoritis suffered deeply because he could find no answer to this question. And yet, we see him, especially during his son's illness, develop a fatalistic resignation of spirit, something like the stoic *ataraxia*, which enabled him to endure life's last agonies without losing his faith. Valaoritis' doubts never became premises from which he could draw metaphysical conclusions, at least not in his poetry. His nihilism, deeply ingrained in him since the days of his youth when he studied Hugo and Byron, was tempered by his Christian belief in the immortality of the soul—a belief that he still clung to even after all the onslaughts of fate. But death, as Palamas observed, opened before him a vision of the whole and put him occasionally in a philosophical mood: "The simple, robustlike form of his poetry widened till it touched the essence of thought; and one can always remember that the boundaries of the heart of a poet are broader than commonly believed."[1]

The poems of this period, which include some translations from the French and Italian,[2] are not arranged chronologically in the Maraslis edition, and few of them bear their dates, although the time of their composition may be inferred from the events described or from accompanying notes and letters. Only the most significant of these will be discussed here—in particular those that have relevance to the development of Valaoritis' thought and his poetic technique.

I *More Patriotic Poems: "The Rock and the Wave" and "To Patriarch Gregorios"*

Following the publication of *Mnemosyna* and *Kyra Phrosyni*, Valaoritis became so immersed in political activity that he wrote very little, if anything, between the years 1859 and 1863. Actually, the first poem written after the above collections was composed on the occasion of the visit of young King George to Corfu after his coronation, in May 1864. "Dedication to King George I" is a political poem, employing familiar allegorical devices meant to suggest that the king embodies qualities of strength and leadership needed to stir the Greeks into appropriate national action. Another poem of this kind, "Twenty-Fifth of March," honors the Annunciation of the Virgin and at the same time celebrates Greece's national holiday. The "Virgin" in this case is identified with Greece, in chains for centuries, awaiting the "Angel" to announce her freedom:

> Awake, arise, fear not, joy to you, Virgin, rejoice,
> My Lord is with you, Greece, arise, rejoice!

Though the feeling is genuine, the poem, with its facile rhetoric, falls short of making any but the most superficial of statements. In a similar vein, "A Greeting to Mother Greece," a poem published in Athens in 1864 and read to various audiences throughout Greece, praises the union of the Heptanese with the mother country. It is loose and loquacious, though rousing and passionate, more of a patriotic speech than a poem.

By contrast, "The Rock and the Wave" has both a strong patriotic theme and some originality in the conception of its central imagery. It was written in March 1863, and published in a newspaper in Corfu, in celebration of the impending union of the seven islands with Greece. This is Valaoritis' most patently allegorical poem, having the standard Valaoritic traits developed to an extreme—a clear and simple, but effective and striking, allegory; a direct and forceful patriotic theme; flowing and thunderous demotic language; ringing, if somewhat ordinary, phrases. With the exception of the "Hymn to Liberty," of Solomos, this is the poem that has appealed, more than any other, to the imagination and patriotic feelings of Greeks.

The poem centers on two symbolic images—the rock and the wave. The former is strong, powerful, arrogant; the latter, humble, servile, seemingly impotent. But the wave finally rises from its lowly state and, raging with suppressed indignation, swells against the rock, hurling insults: "Stand aside, rock," it cries, "and let me pass! ... Out of my way! my soul, once cold and timid, is now a raging blast!" The anger, the passion for freedom, the cry of an enslaved people, "fearful, cowardly, prostrating themselves before a tyrant for centuries but now

striking him down," can be heard in the moan of the wave.
The two central images do, in fact, raise this poem to the level
of the universal; here is the cry of all oppressed peoples, of all
those who, tired of their own bondage and infamy, rise again—
enraged—to strike down a tyrant:

> Stand aside, rock, and let me pass! The slave's foot
> Will trample on your neck. I have awakened a lion!

The dramatic clash between the two is heightened when the
rock replies with its expected derisive and arrogant manner.
But the wave will not be stopped. With an enormous sweep, it
crashes on the rock—which comes down in hideous ruin. When
calm returns, blue and white foam "dance joyously over the
tomb."

This poem, representative of the best of Valaoritis as it is,
suffers somewhat from its own virtues. It is too forceful and
rhetorical to be fine verse. The subject matter is overwhelming,
the voice too loud. It reads like the sermon of a fanatic preacher
delivered to an overzealous audience. As is usual with most
of his patriotic poems, Valaoritis has used excessive rhetoric at
the expense of the finer art of his poetry. But it was a triumph
of rhetoric, and when the poem was read aloud, even his
reserved critics felt swept by the thunder and lightning of the
words of the Lefkadian bard.

Another poem that has had an enormous popular appeal is
"To the Statue of Patriarch Gregorios V." In a way, it is considered a milestone in Greek letters, for it was the first major
Greek poem written in the demotic to be recited in public; it
added immensely to the fame and prestige of Valaoritis. But
in spite of its popularity—and perhaps because of it—this poem
has had little success with Greek critics. In fact, as soon as the
poem was published in 1872, it became the object of violent
attacks by Dimitrios Vernardakis and other poets and critics of
the Heptanesiac School.[3] Sympathetic commentators on the work
of Valaoritis, such as Palamas and Sikelianos, have refrained
from uttering damaging remarks, but they have not praised the
poem either. But some critics feel that the poem has importance
in a historical sense; its great success when it was recited in
public demonstrates without doubt that the Greeks were ready

and eager to hear poetry written in an idiom they could understand.[4]

The poem, recounting the story of the hanging of Patriarch Gregorios by a Turkish mob at the outset of the War of Independence in 1821, is worth studying because it reveals a certain strategy on the part of Valaoritis concerning his political aims. Many of his patriotic poems embody a lesson, usually in the form of praise of a martyr's sacrifice, intending to arouse the audience from apathy into a feeling of intense patriotism that will then lead to action. When Valaoritis had the opportunity to recite his poems to an audience, his intent regarding the poem's effectiveness was identical with that of a speech delivered to the national assembly or to other wider audiences. The poems with patriotic themes are in reality poeticized speeches; many of them have the rhetorical excesses that mark parliamentary orations, and most of such poems are meant to be recited or sung. Valaoritis could not have ignored the opportunity that this poem presented, and he made full use of it.

As the poem begins one thinks of the poet standing in front of the statue just after it was unveiled, addressing its "shadow" and asking a series of adroitly phrased and swiftly moving questions—"Why do you stare at us? Where is your mind flying?"—intended to enliven the "mute stone" and make it respond. But one implied question—What is the meaning of the hanging?—cannot be answered by the mute statue. The poet himself will not give the answer, but he must deftly lead the audience to imagine it. In response to the hanging of the patriarch, the fighters of the revolution intensified their efforts and threw off the yoke of the oppressor. It was a miracle springing from the "Old Father's" disgrace and torture, bringing a catharsis and a renewed desire for freedom. The poet repeats a key question throughout the poem: "What do you want of us?" Of course, the old patriarch must want what Valaoritis demands of his countrymen: to continue the struggle of liberation of their country begun by the martyrs of the revolution. Could not the patriarch, in his present glorification, his immortality already assured, perform a *second* miracle? "Don't you know," the poet asks, "how much life a single look from you could give, / how many hearts could be inspired? / Why don't you awake?"

The strategy of the poet, then, is to appeal to the "shadow" of the patriarch to recall the story of his martyrdom; to give in summary, but in rousing language, the effects of the martyrdom on the success of the revolution; to call for a new miracle and urge the people of Greece to continue the struggle for the liberation of their unredeemed brethren—the great lifelong desire of Valaoritis. "To the Statue of Gregorios V" is not only a poem of power in which the sublimity of the national ideal is expressed, but also one in which the poetic intentions and the political aims of the poet completely accord.

II *"Astrapoyiannos"*

"Astrapoyiannos" is one of the shorter poems of Valaoritis that has enjoyed great success both with popular audiences and literary critics. Paul Nirvanas has called it "the most perfect poem of Valaoritis in essence and in form, a poem for every time and place, a work of art."[5] I. M. Panayotopoulos finds that "Astrapoyiannos," along with "The Escape," are poems of force and power, evoking the feeling of the nightmare. The first poem, as Panayotopoulos puts it, "touches us, and we hear in it the cry from a human heart."[6] Angelos Sikelianos praises the poem with great enthusiasm, comparing it with a scene painted on a Greek vase, "where Achilles was tenderly dressing the wounds of his friend Patroclos." The bond between Lambetis and Astrapoyiannos is a "wondrous heroic friendship, in which the romantic and classic elements meet with a harmony purely Greek."[7] Palamas calls the poem "the best example of a harmonious cooperation of the romantic heart and historical imagination of Valaoritis." In order to understand the poem properly, one must hear it "recited whole."[8]

Published with *Athanasis Diakos* in the spring of 1867, "Astrapoyiannos" was written under extraordinary circumstances. Sitting outside his villa at Madouri in the summer of 1866, and while actually working on the manuscript of *Diakos,* Valaoritis was seized by a sudden inspiration. Without rising from his chair, he wrote the entire poem with pencil on his marble table, not even interrupting to go into the house to get pen and paper. Though extemporaneously composed, the poem does not lack concrete historical content. As Valaoritis shows in his notes to the fourth canto of *Diakos*,[9] Astrapoyiannos, the hero of the poem, was a chieftain who lived in the eighteenth century and who rose, through his personal bravery, to the rank of armatolos of Doris at Sterea Hellas. He performed deeds of such great bravery and valor that he was immortalized in popular ballads. The action of the poem is based on a real incident. Mortally wounded in battle, Astrapoyiannos begs his faithful comrade and foster son, Lambetis, to sever his head from his body and take it to a place of burial, rather than leave it behind, a prey to the enemy. Faced with such a terrible task, Lambetis hesitates. But there is no time to lose; the footsteps of the enemy are heard and the old man, still alive, begs his friend to decapitate him. The "scintillating blade" flies up and down—the head is severed. Lambetis places it in his sack, next to his loaf of bread, and takes to his heels, "fifty enemies pursuing him."

The story of the chase is given in quick bursts of breathless verse. Language, rhythm, imagery combine to give a narrative of superbly rapid action filled with scenes of horror, idyllic descriptions of nature, and pictures of a human mind that slowly disintegrates under the impact of conflicting emotions. Lambetis is chased relentlessly for days and nights, running through wood and dale, treading on mud and snow, stopping to fight, protecting as best as he can the sacred relic he is carrying in his sack. He stops occasionally to rest under a shady tree, or near a fountain. He then takes the sack down from his shoulders, looks at the head, seeing,

> A calm smile on the old man's lips,
> Pale like the moon's rays on a tombstone. . . .

For a moment, Lambetis thinks that the old man is alive, actually standing near him. He washes the head, combs its hair, puts his arms around it, embracing it and kissing it. He slices his bread in half, giving the old man a portion to eat and keeping the rest for himself. In a long, passionate speech, he begs the old man to "awake" and behold the beauteous dawn, the cool waters falling from rock to rock, the haunts in the woods and mountains they used to frequent together.

As he talks, he hears a dog barking in the distance. The enemies are coming; Lambetis takes to his heels again. He runs for days, hungry, for he refuses to eat his "friend's" bread. Wild animals and ravenous birds smell the rotting head and try to snatch it from him; he chases them away. He finally reaches a cave where he sits down and unloads, still holding on to the relic. Exhausted, he falls into a deep sleep and dreams. This is a scene of horror, powerfully, although somewhat theatrically, rendered:

> He stands before him, his eyes hollow,
> The flesh falling into bits—his lips a canyon. . . .

Astrapoyiannos is bitter because he had gone unburied for so long. His face has grown ugly—and he complains that he is unfit to be seen in this state by his beloved trees, the pines and beeches, the gurgling cool fountains, the heights, and the ravines. Gravely, he orders Lambetis to find a place to bury the head, so that his soul can be at rest.

Lambetis awakes and obeys, burying the head, the old man's weapons and the bread, which is still uneaten. Then he returns to fight in the mountains, taking his former chieftain's rank. He too becomes famous and kills scores of enemies. But he is finally wounded, and knows he will soon die. He drags himself to the cave, where his friend is buried. He falls on the grave, just outside the mouth of the cave. The snow falls at night, covering the two heroes.

The poem is written in a variety of metrical patterns which fit the changing psychological moods and follow the dictates of the action. The first eight stanzas are of four lines (abab) of eleven syllables, alternating with ten-syllable iambic lines. This section describes the last moments of Astrapoyiannos, as he begs his friend to cut off his head; it also describes the decapitation, in quick bursts of rhythm. Two stanzas of unrhymed fifteen-syllable lines follow, describing the severed head in its last agony and the decision of Lambetis to flee with it. There are eight stanzas of eleven-syllable lines describing the flight of Lambetis; three stanzas of rhyming fifteen-syllable lines depicting Lambetis washing and "feeding" the head; eleven stanzas of

eleven-syllable lines; fifteen stanzas of troachaic tetrameter in
which the beat quickens considerably, rendering vividly the
final breathless flight of Lambetis; and twenty-six more stanzas
of eleven-syllable lines rounding off the poem. This variation of
rhythm is thus very suggestive of the pace of action. The clatter
of sound, the crisp imagery, the flow of words, are factors that
reflect the enormity of the task they describe and can be fully
appreciated only if one were to follow the advice of Palamas
and try to "recite the poem whole."[10] But the average reader
might find the poem perhaps a bit too long, the speeches of
Lambetis and the "ghost" of the old man unduly wordy. The
poem's single flaw is, in fact, its long-windedness. But in spite
of that fact, it is clear that "Astrapoyiannos" sprang directly
from the heart of the poet, a composition that demonstrates at
once the highest achievement and the limits of Valaoritis' art.

III   The Poems of Death; Other Poems

Several poems were written in the late 1860's and early 1870's
on the subject of death. Most of these were written in lieu of
condolence letters to various friends and relatives of Valaoritis,
or in response to the private grief of a father who had lost a
daughter or a son. Some of these are fine elegies of delicate
texture, showing a lyrical side in Valaoritis which had remained
dormant during the feverish moments of epic composition. Here
we hear the anguished cry of a man who broods over a subject
as ordinary and as profound as the loss of a person one is
acquainted with, or a member of one's family. We see the poet
forced out of his usual range of topics, and contemplating death,
"the great Destroyer and Builder."

In "A Visit to the Veretta Family Cemetery," the poet walks
among the tombs of a cemetery in Athens, where members of a
family close to his were recently buried. The tombs, decorated
with flowers, are of exquisite beauty. Suddenly, the poet forgets
the presence of his companion entirely and falls into a trance.
In the stifling aromas coming from roses, acanthuses, and other
flowers, he seems to be "transported to Heaven, where the
Second Coming is at hand." As angels flutter about, he sees in
a vision two shooting stars sparkling in the distance; they are

his lost daughters, both named Maria, who died in infancy. The poet awakes, sees his companion—a member of the Veretta family—and they both stoop to kiss the tombs. The poem's vivid imagery and pathos show Valaoritis in an intimate mood in which the great anguish of his soul due to the loss of his young daughters is revealed. At the same time, we see that these losses, initially private griefs, gradually wax into a universal sorrow, enabling the poet to share his pain, to understand, and to endure it.

Another poem of this kind, "On the Tomb of Markos Flambouriaris," again refers to a bereaved father but this time over the loss of a son. Markos died at Zakynthos, while his father, who had heard of his son's illness, had hastened to be near him but failed to reach him in time. The poem describes the father over the grave of his son, while a priest is reading a memorial service. No one else is allowed to be present. The father kneels and prays, complaining bitterly about the preference of death for the young and the handsome; why couldn't he, himself, have died instead? The poet interferes at this point, commenting upon the silence of the tomb, the futility of the father's prayer. "Death has no heart," he says in a choruslike comment. The priest puts out the censer. "Let us go, my son," he says, weeping. "Here you can find no consolation. . . . Death is bitter, life a poison."

"On the Death-Bed of Stephanos Messalas, Only an Adolescent" further illustrates Valaoritis' preoccupation with the subject of the death of young people. Undated, the poem vaguely refers to the death of this young man who died at Lefkas, "away from his native country," as a note from the poet tells us. Here there is no narrative, the poet speaking only in metaphorical terms. Death is depicted as a fierce ploughman, driving hard-breathing black oxen ahead of him. He is merciless in goading them; nothing can stand in their path; everything is overturned and uprooted. "And you," the poet asks a young tree, "how do you think you could stand in his way? What brought you there, away from your mother's bosom?" The young man hears the voice and responds from inside the grave. "The tomb is no desolation; it is life and love." But Death doesn't stop ploughing; sleepless, he works day and night. Another young shoot stands in his way; he pays no attention; he uproots it and goes on, smiling mutely.

Valaoritis wrote another poem on the subject of death when Julia Rallis, his nephew's young wife, died of typhus in Vienna with shocking abruptness, only a few months after her wedding. "On the Death of Julia Rallis, October 1874," is one of his best funeral odes, "one of his loveliest poems," according to his son, John. The poem is symbolic rather than merely allegorical, since its metaphors can be read without reference to the particular event. There is evidence here of the broadening and deepening of Valaoritis' means of imaginative conception of death. More persistently now than at any other time he asks the question that haunted him throughout the later part of his career: Why do the young die? Is it possible that death can be seen also as a constructive force? These questions are, of course, not asked in such abstract terms; they are rather woven into the structure of the myth. A myrtle tree (symbolic of youth) goes to the "love's fountain" to "bathe her leaves." But Death, the "harvester," is lurking about the place, pretending to be up early to gather flowers. Like Pluto, his counterpart in the pagan underworld, he uses seductive words to persuade her to go with him: "Come, fresh flower, do not fear, / I command much where you shall be mistress of the blossoms. / Human tears will keep you young, your beauty will be sought." And he adds a line, which has remained famous in the poetry of Valaoritis: "Although I am Death the spoiler, I am also Death the builder."[11] Death succeeds in winning her over with his soft words; neither tears nor laments can bring her back. She has vanished like a star at dawn.

The most famous of the poems of death is the one Valaoritis dedicated to his daughter Nathalia, who died suddenly in Venice in October 1875. "On the Death of my Daughter Nathalia" is a simple and direct poem, a cry from a father's anguished heart. No allegory is woven here; the poet does not seek the advantage of a myth. He expresses his emotion simply, without the paraphernalia of romantic rhetoric. Only the simplest device is used: a contrast which will bring the poet's emotion out more sharply. His great sorrow comes at a time of great natural beauty. This device is familiar in the

poetry of Valaoritis, especially when he describes a young
person's death. It is autumn, the weather warm and pleasant
after the first rains, the flowers are in bloom once more. Bidding
adieu, departing summer scatters about greenery, fragrances,
flowers. Is this the time for a young girl to envy "the tomb's
bedecking," "the sterile darkness of the grave?" Is this the
time for a funeral?

The lines in this poem are some of the most concise Valaoritis
ever wrote, the imagery vivid, the detail concrete and accurate.
This short elegy is undoubtedly one of Valaoritis' finest poems,
consisting of only two eight-line stanzas with a four-line stanza
of rhyming couplets adding a philosophical comment at the
end. This is the only part of the poem which contains a metaphor,
a sharply pessimistic passage, unusual in its sweeping gloom
about the fleeting nature of life:

> Once, a traveller stood near the sea,
> Hurrying, impatient like the breeze.
> The footprint stayed on the sand for a while;
> Then the wave came and brushed it away.

Of the remaining poems written during Valaoritis' later years,
a few are worth mentioning. "First of March, or the Swallow,"
written in 1876, shows Valaoritis hoping against hope during
his declining years at Madouri that the Greeks would again
be aroused by their consciences and continue the national war
of liberation. The swallow, he explains in a letter to P. Chiotis,
"a most graceful bird, is for the Greek not only the herald of
spring and the messenger of joy, the family friend, but its coming in March also marks the beginning of battle against our
traditional enemies" (Maraslis, II, p. 222). The poem is composed with Valaoritis' usual loquacity and fervor of spirit, and
contains more than a few memorable lines. What kind of news
has the swallow brought? "We," he says, meaning all Greeks,
"are afflicted by a terrible apathy, which has paralyzed our
soul. Our lives are sterile like the barren sea, which swells
and vomits dead weed." The bird, then, must perform a service:
it must fly and spread the message that spring does not merely
mean clear waters, green clover, and shepherds' pipes, but war

and roaring rifles. Angrily, the poet dismisses the "eunuchs," who refuse to hear his call to arms. The swallow must fly to the old haunts and rouse the klephts from their slumber, so they can come back and continue the war for freedom.

Another poem that vividly illustrates Valaoritis' worship of the heroes of the revolution is "Kanaris," written on the occasion of the death of Kanaris in 1877. Constantine Kanaris, the famous admiral of the Greek fleet which had once set the Turkish flagship on fire, had lived almost to the age of ninety and had become prime minister four times in postwar Greece. To Valaoritis, Kanaris was a revered fighter, embodying the ideals of Greek heroism in a double sense: while the heroes sung in *Mnemosyna* could only provide inspiration from their graves and needed a poet to remind the nation of their feats, Kanaris had lived on after the War of Independence to give living proof of those old virtues. By writing this poem, Valaoritis had an opportunity to express his admiration for an authentic hero of the revolution as well as to add one more figure to his pantheon of heroes to be worshipped and emulated by modern Greeks.

"Kaloyiannos," meaning "Robin-red-breast," or "Good-John," is one of the most familiar and most popular poems of Valaoritis. Because of his friendly ways, as Valaoritis explains in a note preceding the poem, the bird (*motacilla grisea*) acquired the Greek name *kaloyiannos,* a word that signifies good nature. The poem was written in October 1878, when Valaoritis, weak in health and disappointed by Greece's failure to acquire Epirus, was spending long, lonely hours at Madouri. The song of the bird gave him some pleasant moments which broke the monotony of his days and relieved his anguish. Composing the poem was a way of showing his gratitude to the bird. Fairly short (only thirty-six lines), and written in the usual fifteen-syllable line, the poem develops a central allegorical image. A carefree bird, Kaloyiannos leads a hardy life, content and frugal in his simple habits. He usually begins his song as the sun begins to rise every morning. An eagle that flies overhead is contrasted with the simple and innocent robin. The trophies won by the eagle in his bloody battles with other animals have turned his head. But the robin is not envious; he is content to live his simple life, away from blood, cruelty, and rapine. The only thing he steals occasionally is a heart. "You are stained with blood," he says to the eagle. "I am washed with dew."

Kaloyiannos is indeed a merry fellow; but don't let that deceive you, the poet comments. His life's story is tragic; an "unhealed wound" is hidden deep in his heart. Once he had loved a little she-robin he had met during one of his trips through the forest. Like him, she too was poor. They had built their nest inside a tree, far from the crowd's eyes. With song and love they slowly brought up their children. But one night, as he "held her tight in his arms," he saw a horrifying reptile ready to swallow up their brood. He fainted and did not see the carnage. In the morning, he saw the snake sleeping under the tree, its coils distended, filled up with his children. His mate was dead in the bush. As he embraced her for the last time, her blood stained his chest. That is how he got his red spot.

Aside from its intense lyrical mood and fine versification, the poem is undoubtedly one of the most personal written by Valaoritis. No other poem reflects his life's story more completely. The robin is clearly Valaoritis himself, the red spot representing the wound he received with the loss of his children. But the allegory is broader; the bird also symbolizes the people, the simple, uaffected countrymen whom the poet loved so much. Their speech, like the warble of Kaloyiannos, is simple and unaffected. The contrast of the robin with the eagle helps to underscore the difference between the lowly and the proud, between the arrogant and tyrannical and the humble and good-hearted. It may also reflect the poet's retreat from politics and power into a life of humble obscurity.

In his later years, Valaoritis wrote numerous short lyrics, some of which were dedicated to ladies of his social circle, praising their beauty, grace, or virtue. Most of these poems are commonplace and the product of social convention rather than of art. Valaoritis was a well-bred gentleman of European manners and was always tactful and complimentary to the ladies of Athens and Lefkas, many of whom admired and worshipped him. Eloisia, his wife, tolerated this admiration good-naturedly, and her husband, who seemingly never went beyond the limits of propriety, occasionally teased her in his letters about his "adventures." Of these poems worth mentioning is "Roxani Soutsos," a poem of two six-line stanzas wherein Roxani, an Athenian lady, is compared to a rose and a lily, flowers sought out by the bee, presumably the poet, or perhaps another admirer of the lady's beauty. In another poem, "To Chariklea S.," the poet is likened to an old plane tree that has suffered the ravages of time and is now at a disadvantage when compared to the young blooming saplings growing around him. It is in such a group of poems that we find the admirable "Agrambeli" ("The Wild Vine"), one of the outstanding lyric poems of Valaoritis. The familiar romantic contrast is employed here: a pretty wild vine is attempting to resist the seductive words of a mighty plane tree growing above her, and trying to convince her to "abandon" the lowly earth and climb up to his height. He promises to make her "an empress," with a tiara and a throne. She is finally convinced, leans upon the strong tree, climbs up and is lost into its thick branches. "A pity," cries the poet, "that for a little height, my blond vine, you gave up your purity...." Many years after the poet's death, an old woman confessed to her friendly grocer that she indeed was the lady, alluded to as "wild vine," who was seduced in her youth while working as a maid in the poet's household at Madouri.[12]

CHAPTER 6

Photeinos

THOUGH left unfinished, *Photeinos* is Valaoritis' masterpiece, the work that more than any other represents the mature expression of both his poetic technique and his highest ideals. With *Photeinos*, Valaoritis finally answers his call as a poet fully, writing a poem that most certainly ensures him a position as a master of modern Greek and a poet of high rank. The reader of the works of Valaoritis in the original will find many passages of great beauty, particularly where the Greek landscape is described; in *Photeinos*, such exquisite attainments can be found in almost every line. It is a poem where language, imagery, ideas are masterfully fused into a perfect whole. It is a work written with the assurance of a master who has finally conquered his medium—of a man who has understood and accepted his mission. On the surface, *Photeinos* is a rustic drama, a poem of action like his previous major poems, of epic breath and proportion. It tells the story of a farmer, an ex-fighter, who has received an affront at the hands of his Venetian master and is planning revenge. In reality, it is a story where Valaoritis expresses his love for his native land, his long-suppressed desire for action, his ideal of freedom embodied in a heroic old man— representative of the people, poet and father telling his ultimate secrets.

I Background and Technique

Photeinos was written during the last year of Valaoritis' life, when he was in poor health and broken in spirit over his son's illness. He wrote at intervals, from February till June, only when the news from Madeira was favorable. Understandably, this poem was not planned with the same meticulous care exhibited when Valaoritis wrote his earlier major works. Aside from a

129

glossary (not comparing in extent and detail to that of *Diakos*) attached to the end of the poem, and a brief discussion of it in a letter to his wife, he left no notes, no preface or introduction, as he usually did, to explain his purpose, plan, and poetic theories. The poem was left unfinished, progressing only to its third canto, and the poet was obviously unable to put the finishing touches to what he had already written.

In designing *Photeinos*, Valaoritis evidently remained faithful to his principle, expressed earlier,[1] that modern Greek poetry must have history as its basis. However, the subject matter of his last poem was drawn, not from the recent events of the Revolution of 1821, but from an obscure incident which took place in the fourteenth century, when western Greece was under the rule of Venice. In 1357, the people of Lefkas rose against the oppressive Venetian overlord, George Gratzianos, defeated him at the battle of Episkopi, and took him prisoner. The data for this incident were derived from an article by the German scholar, C. Hopf, which Valaoritis had read in the translation of I. A. Romanos.[2] Though the basis for the poem thus remains firmly historical, Valaoritis innovated for the first time in a major work by inventing not only the main figure, Photeinos, but all the minor characters with the exception of Gratzianos. He also invented the larger portion of his plot. This departure from historical detail regarding both plot and character may account for the poem's liveness and superior dramatic quality—achieved without compromise on the essential point that Greek poetry must be at the service of national aims. As there were no notes left explaining the poet's reasons for choosing a topic so remote from Greece's recent past, one can only surmise that he intended a parallel between the Byzantine period and the heroic era of the Revolution of 1821. The medieval uprising described in *Photeinos* shares the same basic character with all Greek struggles throughout the centuries: it was a struggle to throw off the oppressive yoke of a foreign invader. The veracity of the poem's historical background thus substantiates the author's claim that Greek history must be viewed as a whole, as a series of heroic episodes in the struggle against oppression and tyranny since ancient times.

Photeinos represents a shift not only in chronology, but also

in the poet's national and political orientation. Writing at the
end of his life, when dreams of a political career had subsided,
but still hoping against hope that Greece would manage a
satisfactory settlement of the borders of Epirus, Valaoritis
launched with this last major work a bifocal attack against forces
both internal and external. With its basically nationalistic content, it would serve as a bugle call to arouse the slumbering
sentiments of Greeks, prompting them to another struggle to
free the still enslaved Greek lands. This objective was in harmony with previously stated aims of his poetry. But the external
enemy of Greece is no longer the Turk alone. Gratzianos, the
villain of *Photeinos*, is a Venetian, a westerner. Symbolically,
he represents the Franks, the mighty powers of Europe who
had recently betrayed Greece's interests in the treaties of Berlin
and San Stefano (1878). Photeinos, the hero of the poem, an
ex-fighter who has settled into a quiet life of farming, takes up
arms to avenge a humiliating insult he has suffered at the hands
of his lord, Gratzianos. Photeinos is Valaoritis himself, emerging
from the ashes of his isolation to take up "arms"—his poetry—
to wield a blow against the powerful, who play games with
the fortunes of the small. No Homeric objectivity distinguishes
this poem. *Photeinos,* as Palamas remarks, "is full of nervously
vibrating hatred against the oppressor. This feeling of complaint,
of bitterness, of anger against the strong of Europe . . . this is
the feeling that *Photeinos* conveys."[3]

Another remarkable innovation in *Photeinos* is a radical change
of the locale from the mainland of Greece, the scene of his
major narrative poems, to Lefkas, the island of his birth. Epirus
and Sterea Hellas had so far been the renowned centers of
action in the War of Independence, the places where the clang
of arms had been heard, where the great sacrifices for freedom
were made. Deeply conscious of their symbolic significance and
national importance, Valaoritis used Jannina and Alamana as
the centers of the action of his two major poems, *Phrosyni* and
Diakos. But, as he was nearing the end of his career and conflicting feelings and emotions overwhelmed him, he chose for
the action of his last poem the place that he knew best, perhaps
as a sign of the respect and affection he held for his fellow
citizens, as his son John Valaoritis explains.[4] He had lived in the

island most of his life; he knew the inhabitants, their customs, habits, speech. He had studied their idioms minutely, taking diligent notes. He had attended their funerals, weddings, baptisms; he had known their joys and sorrows; he had become *laós*—the people—one of them, like his protagonist, *Photeinos*. This fact perhaps explains why *Photeinos* was written with the certainty and authority of one who knows his subject matter thoroughly. The poet here steps on totally familiar ground and shows himself a complete master of his craft. *Photeinos*, as John Valaoritis puts it, "is an art gallery of vivid, brilliant natural colors, painted with the power of a Rembrandt— and has the descriptive precision one finds in domestic events."[5]

Finally, *Photeinos* is a poem of family relationships. Photeinos has a son, Mitros, his helper in the fields and second in command in the planned battle against the Franks; he also has a seventeen-year-old daughter, Thodoula, whom he treats with deep affection. She is about to be married to Lambros, a young man, son of Floros, his friend and old collaborator in the fights for freedom. The entire atmosphere of the poem, especially in the second and third cantos, is domestic, the tone subdued and free from the excess of rhetoric, the events familiar and reflecting everyday life. The language is concrete, though highly idiomatic and topical. Despite the dithyrambic passages of the first canto, where Photeinos proudly faces his master, the poem on the whole offers a harmonious and somewhat idyllic picture of common people living the ordinary routine of everyday life in a somewhat romanticized Greek province.

II   *Plot Analysis of* Photeinos

Canto I. The poem begins abruptly, plunging the reader directly into the action. In a much admired half line, Photeinos urges Mitros, his son, to "take a lump of earth" and chase away "those dogs" which are spoiling his seed beds. Hesitating, Mitros points out that the dogs belong to the Venetian overlord, Gratzianos, who is out on a hunting expedition with his bodyguard. Enraged with his son's timidity, Photeinos leaps like a youth, grabs a rock, and hurls it with his sling at the dogs; he hurts one, kills another, cursing the "loathsome Franks," and chiding his son for his loss of nerve. A strong youth, who "could squeeze granite in his hand," Mitros should not be afraid: "The slave stores up fat; he has no blood, no soul."

Wisely, Mitros points out that to be brave at such a moment is foolish; a whole army is against them—two men. To be sure, Gratzianos and his men are approaching fast, riding over sown fields, demolishing fences, tearing down everything in their path. A horseman is seen riding ahead, holding a spear, trampling on the planted seeds. The old man stands before him, undaunted. Other horsemen draw near. The poet describes old Photeinos in vivid, chiseled imagery:

> His head all white; the beard thick, long,
> Running down his sunburnt chest like foam . . .
> Like the blooming honeysuckle falling from a rock.
> Years of slavery, time's merciless plough
> Had furrowed his forehead, carved it deep. . . .

Photeinos is one of the many admirable old men frequently found in the poetry of Valaoritis. They are all sturdy, high-spirited, unbending before the conqueror.

Valaoritis describes the old man's former life as a warrior, then returns to the action. Another horseman emerges from the mist and speaks:

> "Old fool, was it you who threw rocks at my dogs?"
> "Myself, and no other."
> "Speak more respectfully. . . . Lower your head, bend
> your knee before your master. Tramp! Beggar!"

It is Gratzianos; he strikes the old man with his spear, but Photeinos stands firm, refusing to bow his head, answering the rider defiantly. Gratzianos delivers a haughty, self-indulgent speech, abusing the old man and the Greeks, "who have grown decrepit," but don't mean to die and "rid the world of their presence." They are a disgrace to their noble ancestors. Here Photeinos rises to give a memorable answer:

> "If the branches seem dry, the root is always green, . . . This ox, which looks calm and mellow, when goaded can fly into a rage and tear you down. This is what they call the people. . . ."

For a long time now, Photeinos has endured slavery patiently; his property is overtaxed, his profits taken. No law protects him.

Gratzianos demands an apology for his wounded dogs, but Photeinos answers back defiantly: "Better be hanged than kneel before you!"

Gratzianos orders his men to take the old man's oxen away. Two of them do so; two others arrest the rebellious old man and place his open palm on the handle of a plough and stab it with their blades. Blood stains the handle, dripping down to the earth in runnels. The men laugh savagely. Mitros has fallen down, moaning in agony and shame. But the "old dragon" does not stir, nor does he utter a word. But in a flash memories of his old deeds come back to haunt his mind; once more he becomes the fierce warrior that he was a long time ago. In his mind, he already begins to plan his revenge.

Canto II. The scene shifts to the domestic atmosphere of Photeinos' cottage, which is built on a rock on the precipitous slope of Mt. Kondros, rising on the east side of the fertile valley of Sphakiotes, a village cluster in the middle section of Lefkas. The description of the interior of the cottage shows much knowledge of topical nomenclature. Valaoritis writes in terse, euphonious lines, master of his craft in the tradition of Theocritus and Homer:

> Four walls, all white, a chicken coop, a stable,
> The pen for sheep, a dozen beehives,
> A wide, clean yard, double-girded with stones around,
> Where the smilax climbed, thick, green, profuse,
> Honeysuckle, myrtle, gay artemesia added cool-shaded
>   blossoms. . . .

Such is the kingdom of the poor man. From the top of Mt. Kondros Photeinos liked to gaze at the sea spreading out in the distance, always beautiful in its illusory, ever-changing colors. The image of the sea assumes for a moment the familiar Valaoritic allegorical dimensions: calm and tame, caressing the sea shore, the sea resembles enslaved Greece. But she can be wild and stormy, raging furiously, like a rebel that rises against the oppressor. She is a Greek sea! She cannot suffer the foreigner's arrogant prow furrowing her waters.

A lengthy passage follows in which we are told of Photeinos' past, of his early apprenticeship to a wise monk who had escaped the persecution of the Turks at Constantinople and had settled in these parts, practicing medicinal cures and leading an exemplary ascetic life. A sort of "pharmakos," he could exorcise evil spirits, protecting sown fields from locusts, and curing animals of skin diseases. Photeinos, who had entered the monastery as a novice, followed the holy man in his search for alms around the villages, and he was taught stories from him that stirred his imagination and "washed away the dust" that had gathered on every slave's soul. In his mature years, Photeinos could recall the past history of Greece, such glorious events as the defeat of Xerxes at Salamis, the sea battle at Actium, the building of Nicopolis by a Roman emperor—the first in a series of such monuments, for Greece was to remain enslaved for many centuries.

The cottage of Photeinos is next described in rich detail: arms are hanging on the walls, bows and arrows, a sword, a belt, a carved axe. The "sleepless flame," an oil lamp, burns in front of the icon of the Resurrection. He has made vows, dedicating these weapons to the fight for liberty. There is a description of domestic items—weaving utensils, a kneading trough, the spinning wheel, a spindle, wool, thread, an oil lamp stand in the corner, the trousseau pack with the plaited woolen blanket. All these the poet describes intimately in their idiomatic peasant terminology, giving his text concreteness and authenticity. This is a prosperous farmer's household. On the roof rafts swallows build their nests every spring, bringing messages of life, hope, and happiness.

Photeinos has one daughter left unmarried, the lovely Thodoula, "his sweet last child." Not yet seventeen, she is like a "wild flower of the valleys," a balm "fresh and cool" to heal the old man's wounded heart. With a song she weaves on the loom, with a song she carries water from the fountain at Phryas. She works in the fields, hoeing, harvesting, helping with the sheepfold. Wherever she goes, she brings freshness and laughter:

A dewdrop of morning; joy, joy to the lips
That will drink her with a kiss!

It is late March, snowing outside; winter has lingered on
late this year. Urging his daughter to kindle the fire so that his
cold feet will get warmer, Photeinos recollects his past as a
fighter and his brave forays against the Franks. But "now that
the wolf is old, the dogs bite him," he complains bitterly.

The present is a scene of domestic comfort. Father and
daughter chat pleasantly, whiling away the night. The fire is
blazing before them; it is rich, luxuriant, a symbol of life and
resurrection. Thodoula dresses his wound, which is still unhealed and aching, applying pork fat for balm. Photeinos sighs;
it is already five months since he received the wound, and the
insult is still unwashed. He then begs his daughter to tell him
who she would like to marry; she hesitates while he mentions
various names. She finally says "Yes," when he mentions the
name of Lambros. Lambros, "the wild son of Floros," is noted
for his unruly disposition, his love of knives, his great physical
strength. Photeinos, who secretly admires the young man, gives
his blessing, vowing to "fight better now." Lambros may be
poor, but he has for a treasure his abundant youth and the
love of the people of Lefkas. He will continue the work of
Photeinos.

A knock comes on the door. Covered with snow, the old
warrior, Floros, comes in. The two white-maned old lions
embrace. Photeinos immediately announces that he has given
his consent for the marriage between Lambros and Thodoula,
and Floros hears the news happily. The two men begin their
nocturnal chatter, while Thodoula prepares dinner for them
and then withdraws to her chamber. The canto ends with a
lengthy, rather flowery prayer, a lyric passage describing the
innocence of her sleep and her dreams of a shepherd lover who
leads his flock to pasture near a lovely fountain.

Canto III. This canto begins with four stanzas in which the
poet reverts to his familiar technique of allegorizing to make
his points. The wave of the sea, the wild steed, the boar, the
eagle, we are told, are elements in nature representing youth

and robustness. But, alas! change affects them as it does every-thing else; age soon arrives, and the vigor of youth is lost. Photeinos and Floros, once young and supple-bodied warriors, are now unable to take action; they are simply *talking* about war. "Old age! Old age!" exclaims the poet, briefly interrupting the flow of his narrative to philosophize.

But soon these abstractions about old age and death are aban-doned, and the poet returns to the concreteness of the earlier part of the narrative. The old men continue their talk, and Photeinos brings out his choice wine, "keropati," which is pro-duced from a mixture of purple Patras grapes and the "laurel black" grapes of Lefkas. As Photeinos and Floros enjoy the wine, they good-naturedly discuss the dowry Thodoula is to bring and decide the wedding is to take place in a month, on Sunday after Easter, Apostle Thomas' holiday. The wedding celebration will be the signal for the attack against the Franks.

Photeinos for a moment turns bitter at the thought of the loss of his dear daughter, "the light of his eyes." Another thought oppresses him; how can one expect his children to be happy and enjoy life if they are to remain slaves? Fathers and children are doomed to the same fate: "Worms inside their cocoons, unable to take wing...." In this mood Photeinos reprimands Floros for his merrymaking. But the latter is not to be drawn into his friend's pessimistic disposition; he is not to be shaken in his faith. With firm words he reminds Photeinos that it was he who, a long time ago, had kindled the fire of freedom in the heart of Floros. Together they had fought, had made plans, and had dreamed about seeing their country liberated one day. How is it that Photeinos seems suddenly to have lost his nerve, especially now that the hour of revenge is drawing near?

"A father is grieving for the loss of his daughter," replies Photeinos. "The gift of joy that she brought me was unknown to me before. And the hatred I feel for the enemy has clouded my thinking." Photeinos speaks metaphorically:

By the time the apple in the cypress becomes a tree, the tree a mast to fight a gale, on every rig, many generations will perish.... I know others will live to enjoy the seed I am planting.

Photeinos has now recovered from his momentary faint-hearted-
ness. He is ready to fight.

> "Let us drink, Ktenas. Down with the Franks."
> "Amen. Let their heads become a string of beads,
>   hanging from the branches of your tree."

In his renewed determination, Photeinos wants to know how
his friends in the rear villages took the news of the insult he
received from the enemy—are they ready to fight? "Old and
young came to greet me," Floros assures him. "All are burning
with the desire to see the foreigner go." Photeinos can have as
many men as he wants. A thousand. Photeinos tells him that
he expects to hear from an important chieftain, Nikiforos, who
might add substantially to his support. No matter what the
chieftain does, however, Photeinos will fight. He is not dismayed by the difficulty of the task ahead, though he is "poor,
small, feeble, a lone reed in the plain." But God, who bends the
mighty tree down, will help the little reed to grow.

As the time draws near, Photeinos is aroused; the savagery of
the warrior is awakened in him. But he worries: the Franks
are already suspicious, there may be traitors among their followers, the villagers will suffer rape and pillage. This is the
time to have not only valor, but strength. Too bad he has to
go into battle when no longer young. Sighing deeply, he pro-
ceeds to discuss the coming fight, the possible outcome, the
consequences of it for the future of their children. Quite likely,
their lives will end on the field of battle. Floros asks for one
more sip of wine. They clink their glasses: "Let us have health."
"Easy, Ktenas. Lower your voice. She might awake and hear
us." But Floros assures him that the young sleep soundly. "It is
us, the old, who have before us the picture of the grave," he
adds. Finally, the two friends bid good night to each other.
Floros asks for a last gift; the head of Arnaoutis, a fearsome
manhunter, as a trophy to hang from a tree branch. Photeinos
assures him that he will have it.

The two men sleep light-heartedly; the poet compares them
to the seashore, when the waves have subsided after a gale. The
fire burns in the fireplace, "brilliant, all alive, like the mother

of warriors keeping vigil over her untamed children." The sleeping old men breathe force and power from her mystic strength. She burns bright and flaming, a symbol of undying liberty, transforming them into ferocious fighters. At the other end of the house, a meager oil lamp illumines the serene and hopeful face of Thodoula. A thin partition separates her from the two men; a "chasm" separates the souls of the two generations.

The scene now shifts outside. Imperceptibly and quickly winter changes into spring. The north wind subsides, the night becomes calm and tender. The southern sea brings humid air, the soil of the earth breaks, water oozes from the ground. Springs quietly run. The time has come for an uprising, as the Lefkadians can no longer hold back their hatred against the oppressor or stifle their love of liberty.

Light steps are heard, knocks come on the door. Lamia, the dog, barks. It is Mitros and Lambros, the two young men returning from their mission. They bring news that Nikiforos, the chieftain, will be as good as his promise and will join them on Apostle Thomas' Sunday. There is an outburst of joy as Lambros is informed that he has been chosen by Thodoula. Photeinos tries to calm them down, pointing out that there is yet much to be done; Mitros must depart, to invite the "guests" to the feast; he must be careful to make them swear "a triple oath" that they will keep the secret entrusted to them. Ktenas must take his son and go too, without delay, before dawn. The cocks are already crowing. Photeinos will have no peace until he sees them gone. "I am going, Photeinos," replies Floros, gaily alluding to the empty wine gourd which will enable him to climb lightly the steep slope of Mt. Elati.

III *A Critique of* Photeinos

Hailed as a masterpiece by recent critics, *Photeinos* was not well known by the Greek public until 1891, when it was published for the first time.[6] Roidis, writing only a few months after the death of Valaoritis, does not seem to be aware of the existence of the poem.[7] Even Palamas, in his first article on Valaoritis in 1889, does not mention *Photeinos*. When *Photeinos* was published in Athens in 1891, there was no reaction of any consequence by the critics. John Valaoritis, in his biography of his father, attributes this neglect to "essential changes in ideas and feelings" during modern times, when men "no longer feel kinship for the heroic period," and Greek letters "have been subjected to new influences coming from the West."[8] At the same time, John considers *Photeinos* a more complex poem than his father's previous works, requiring more attention on the part of the reader. This factor may account for its lukewarm reception by the general public and the critics' prolonged neglect.

Photeinos gradually became better known, though it never enjoyed the popular success of the *Mnemosyna* or *Kyra Phrosyni*, or of some of the celebrated short poems, such as "The Rock and the Wave" and "To the Statue of Gregorios V." But those modern critics who have noticed and commented upon the work of Valaoritis as a whole assign *Photeinos* an exceptionally high place. Aside from the criticism of Palamas and Angelos Sikelianos, noteworthy comments have been made by such others as Spiros Melas, Pavlos Nirvanas, and Aristos Kambanis. Recently (1970), *Photeinos* was edited by the distinguished Greek scholar and professor of modern Greek literature at the University of Salonica, G. P. Savidis. This edition, thorough both in its critical and textual approach, easily sets the standards for future editions of Valaoritis' works—a task urgently needed.

Palamas, in his two speeches on Valaoritis to the Athens Educational Club in 1914, was the first scholar to make significant critical remarks on *Photeinos*. This poem, says Palamas, can be seen as the "normal end" of the career of Valaoritis in several respects. It reflects the termination, but also the final act of his political efforts. Disgusted with politics, Valaoritis has retreated to the country, devoting his time to his family and the cultivation of his fields. Photeinos, the hero of his poem, has also given up "fighting" to become a quiet farmer, enjoying the pleasures of a domestic life. But Photeinos, like Valaoritis, is first and foremost a patriot; the insult he receives provides him with the excuse to take up arms again against the oppressor. Valaoritis, in an allegorical sense, also takes up "arms" through the medium of his poetry to once again stir up the imagination of Greece, and to prompt it to heroic action as in former heroic times.⁹ Verse becomes a weapon; in his warrior's hands it shines like a blade, thunders like a musket. But his hands do not tremble, the verse hits directly—no mistake. Unluckily, *Photeinos* remained unfinished. The poem lacks even the finishing touches, but it lacks none of those qualities that distinguish the power, grace, and mastery of Valaoritic art.¹⁰

Photeinos contains another "terminal" quality, says Palamas. It was Valaoritis' "swan song"—a farewell to life and to his family. The presence of Thodoula, Photeinos' daughter, softens the tone of the poem and saves it from the arid harshness of warlike masculinity that pervades the atmosphere of *Diakos*. Thodoula is Photeinos' last child, his most beloved one, the joy and comfort of his age. She is, as Palamas puts it, "The treasure of the heart of a father who lamented the deaths of his Maria and Nathalia, and who kept dreaming secretly of his passing angels; this treasure is spent in this poem."¹¹ As Photeinos is afraid of losing Thodoula by giving her in marriage to Lambros, so Valaoritis fears the loss of Aimilios, who was lying on his sick bed at Madeira. The strong feeling expressed by Photeinos for Thodoula reflects the strong emotion of Valaoritis as he was bidding farewell, through the medium of his poetry, to his absent family.

There is another quality Palamas admires in *Photeinos,* a certain tendency to laughter, merriment, humor; something like a Homeric irony, or "high spirits" (the untranslatable *kéfi*). This is neither biting satire nor a playful disposition, but "something that slides easily from the profound and sublime theme into the familiar domestic talk, finding its own joke; something not easy to embroider into the delicate fabric we call verse; a more or less careless move can tear it."¹² In the third canto of *Photeinos*, the two chieftains are having a good time, imbibing the *keropati,* the delicious red wine, and "in their way reproducing, with their wisely pictorial and vivid language, the state of the popular mind at the eve of an uprising."¹³ There is in this poem "a tight indissoluble bond between the poet's art and the soul of the people," both in meaning and in expression. This makes poetry stop at details, viewing things at a close range, rather than as a whole and from a distance. Valaoritis puts this scheme into action splendidly. Thus the poetry of Valaoritis becomes at the same time a bridge that carries us from verse to prose, from the historical poem to the epic narrative, making us realize (speaking from the point of view of a Greek writer) that there is in "our new literature a march forward, a rhythm, a tradition, something like an evolution, or transformation." With all its obstacles, this road is the proper study for the literary historian.[14]

Of the other critics, Spiros Melas holds that the work of Valaoritis as a whole is a lifelong effort "to rid Greekness of all foreign elements and influences." In *Diakos,* he came close to this objective; more so with *Photeinos,* the subject matter of which reveals a deeper symbolic value. Earlier, he had dealt with the Turkish domination; now, at the end of his life, he waged battle against Frankish rule. "On this matter," Melas says, "Valaoritis remains an example rare, splendid, and unsurpassed in the history of Greek letters. And the haughty, Frank worshipper Roidis should have fitted his eyeglasses better on his nose while looking at this fact."[15]

Aristos Kambanis also finds that *Photeinos* is Valaoritis' best work. This poem, according to Kambanis, does not have the sentimentality of *Phrosyni,* the one-block narrative episode of *Daikos,* the lyrical downpour of "Astrapoyiannos." It has the variety of large compositions—country freshness, an idyllic love affair, warlike fury, dramatic interest, characterization, local color. The story describes the rising of Lefkas against Gratzianos in the fourteenth century. But even though the local element is extolled, we arrive through it at the idea of the common and the universal—the ideal love of one's country. It is a pity that Valaoritis' most mature work remained unfinished.[16]

Pavlos Nirvanas is the only modern critic who is critical of *Photeinos.* Nirvanas admits that with *Photeinos* Valaoritis becomes "master of his art, always of his own art, giving the measure of his mastery in expression, language, verse." But there is "nothing more than this perfection of technique."[17] Valaoritis is tired; "[h]e is no longer the Valaoritis of *Athanasis Diakos,* which, with all its faults, shows the heroic poet in a characteristically psychological note." His hero is a disappointed klepht. He is Valaoritis himself, dejected after the failure of his political struggles. The scenery changes, too; the enemy is no longer the traditional Turk, but the Venetian, who is not capable of inspiring in the soul of the poet the hatred, the instinct for revenge produced by the confrontation between Greek and Turk. One does not fight here defending one's *faith* as well as one's *country*. "Regardless of all these things," Nirvanas adds, "*Photeinos*, in my opinion, in spite of the relative perfection of its form, lacks the intrinsic poetic elements to have become, even if completed, the crown of Valaoritic art. Its hero would not have been able to carry on his shoulders the full weight of a great poem, as its creator imagined it. Its hero, as Mr. Varnalis correctly observes, lacks 'ideal grandeur.' "[18]

Angelos Sikelianos, a fervent apologist for Valaoritis as a man and a poet, finds *Photeinos* the best of all Valaoritis' works.[19] Sikelianos considers Valaoritis' flight from politics, which resulted, among other things, in the composition of *Photeinos*, a salutary move, allowing the poet to "wash away the dirt and dust of the big city."[20] By going to live in the country, the poet escaped "the boredom of fruitless etiquette, the phony protocol of social meetings," coming back again to get in touch with the people's soul. Naked, "like Adam," Valaoritis reentered the place he was born, the original wellspring of his being— Lefkas. He became one with the people.

Photeinos is a remarkable figure. With his characteristic vision, Sikelianos sees him "as the priest of the Eleusinian religion," who is also a fighter, protecting the sacred rights of the people to derive sustenance from their land.[21] He fights for bread and for liberty (*philósophos* and *philopólemos*—lover of wisdom and lover of war—are Eleusinian terms which often have the same meaning). In ancient times, Photeinos would have been called Vouzigis or Echeltos, and would have held in his hand not a spear but an ox goad. The subtitle of Valaoritis' poem is indeed "The Revolution of *Voukentra*," or "ox goad." As Echeltos protected the ancient population against raids of outlaws and invaders, so Photeinos, his modern counterpart, protects the Lefkas people against the abuses of the Venetians.

On the surface, *Photeinos* seems a typical historical country folk story; in essence, it is a universal human epic, the epic "of the complete man of Mother Earth, of the universal man who stands unblemished in the center of creation and of

nature."[22] Photeinos is the man of all places, all geographical
latitudes, the really free man; he tolerates the yoke of the
Venetian overlord, but when his human dignity is abused, he
defies the tyrant, hurls back insults, and incites his fellow
patriots to an uprising. Though a humble peasant, Photeinos
embodies those qualities of character that the Greeks always
held dear. He is a loving and caring father, a diligent worker
in the fields, a lover of history and of the glorious myths of
Greece, and finally and chiefly an independent man. In outlining
these simple virtues, Valaoritis has summed up Greeke *areté*, a
value surviving in the minds of the Greeks since Homer's time.

CHAPTER 7

Valaoritis and His Critics– A Final Estimate

COVERING more than a century, the history of criticism on the work of Valaoritis is interesting in that it exposes the shortcomings of both his poetry and of those who criticized it. It shows on the one hand that the poetry of Valaoritis has triumphantly survived the damage done to it by its detractors, and on the other that it has not yet fully justified the faith placed in it by its apologists. In spite of the plethora of critical opinion, Valaoritis' position in modern Greek letters has not yet been established with finality. For some, he is hardly a poet. ("The greatest success of Valaoritis," wrote John Apostolakis in 1936, "was to convince the Greek public that he was really a poet."[1]) For others, he is a national bard occupying a position as high as that of Solomos. ("Solomos came first after centuries of darkness and silence; he is our father. But that does not mean that Valaoritis was not his child; Valaoritis also stands at his peak, his throne, one of the most honorable in modern Greece," wrote Palamas.[2])

This vacillation of critical opinion, which has caused his reputation to suffer and the final recognition of his achievement to be unduly delayed, can be attributed to several factors. No doubt, some of the early critical hostility, while Valaoritis was still alive, was political in character. Some of his opponents in the Greek National Assembly published libels against him, attempting not only to discredit him as a political figure, but also to damage his reputation as a poet.[3] In 1868, attacks on the poetry of Valaoritis came from a member of the Ionian School and a follower of Solomos, Panayotis Panas, who criticized Valaoritis "for exploiting the technique of the folk songs" and for regarding himself as an equal to Solomos. Another

145

member of the Ionian School, Iakovos Polylas, found the poetry of Valaoritis "crude," "unrefined," its imagery vague and lacking vividness.[4] Polylas, in fact, posed the question—"the fruitless, neo-pedantic dilemma," according to a recent critic—whether Greeks ought to accept Valaoritis, rather than Solomos, as their national poet.[5] The attack of Dimitrios Vernardakis on the poem praising the Patriarch Gregorios, alluded to elsewhere,[6] had an adverse effect on all subsequent criticism, providing a point of departure to those who would dwell on the defects of the poetry of Valaoritis. The Ionian poets and critics, envious of Valaoritis' ascendancy as a national figure, made systematic efforts to exclude Valaoritis from the ranks of the Ionian School by pointedly—and even maliciously—describing the defects of his poetry when compared to that of Solomos.[7] Their efforts have been abundantly rewarded, for twentieth-century critics and scholars have overwhelmingly chosen Solomos as their favorite nineteenth-century poet. The contributions of Valaoritis, on the other hand, remain inadequately defined, his work as a whole unedited and poorly studied, and his poetry oftentimes treated with condescension. Nevertheless, Valaoritis lacks neither supporters among critics nor a wide influence among the Greek public, which has stubbornly refused to cast him into oblivion and still recognizes him as the poet who speaks more directly than any other to the Greek heart.

I *The Criticism of Palamas*

Of all the commentators on the work of Valaoritis, Palamas holds the foremost position. Palamas did not examine the work of Valaoriits in a scholarly fashion; he viewed it as a whole, dwelling on general aspects of poetry, clarifying its relationship to the poetry of the Heptanesiac School—particularly that of Solomos—its influence on subsequent poets, the contributions it made on the prevalence of the demotic idiom in the twentieth century. As has already been shown,[8] Palamas did discuss in some detail the longer works of Valaoritis and made comments on some of the shorter ones; but his approach was that of an at large commentator-critic—one who attempts to establish the position of an author in its general context, rather than one who dwells on particulars. The role of Palamas as a poet-critic resembles somewhat that of T. S. Eliot in the English-speaking world. While examining the past, both men attempted to reappraise the present and to provide standards that would be implemented in more specific ways in the future. The criticism of Palamas on the work of Valaoritis is that of a pioneer—a pioneer sometimes carried away by his enthusiasm. Palamas left the details of the work he started to be done later. Unfortunately, until very recently his example has not been followed.[9]

The earliest article of Palamas on the work of Valaoritis appeared in the periodical *Estia* in 1889, ten years after the death of Valaoritis. Calling him the "rhapsodist of the armatoloi," Palamas found two basic themes in the poetry of Valaoritis: first was the intention of the poet to extol the heroic grandeur of the struggles of the Greek nation to free itself from the foreign yoke; second, the poet attempted through the medium of his poetry to describe "the original beauty of Greek nature." From these two themes emerged, first, his heroic poems, and, second, the shorter lyrics. Other aspects of his work worth studying are the per se literary value of the poems; and the life of the man, indispensable to the understanding of his poetry; also, a measure of his popularity must be taken into account in a correct final estimate of his position in Greek literature.[10]

Valaoritis, according to Palamas, had knowledge of the aims that his poetry should achieve and nearly all his published poems were products of mature deliberation. Before he created his poetry, he created his poetics; all his major poems (excepting *Photeinos*) and many of his shorter ones were prefaced with painstaking introductions. In spite of his boast that he let his imagination "run unbridled wherever it wished," Valaoritis had nothing in common with poetic adventurers: he had clear objectives and a mature judgment; his first serious poetic collection, *Mnemosyna*, came from a man who had completed his thirtieth year, had developed principles about language and poetry, and had taken control of his career. In his writings, Valaoritis combined the poet, the historian, and the patriot. He had discovered that the role best fitting the Greek poet was that of endeavoring to amalgamate the most serious interests of the nation with those of its poetry. Thus for Valaoritis the roles of the poet, political leader, and historian became interchangeable. The largeness of this vision is what makes Valaoritis an indispensable and irreplaceable national leader.

In matters of language, Valaoritis contributed significantly, even more so than Solomos. The latter was unable to exert complete control over his language, "unable to conceive it entirely in its reality."[11] Valaoritis, more happily, took hold of it, "as if it were an untamed colt, and managed to tame it and bridle it to the degree required."[12] Valaoritis believed in the language of the common people, frequently stating in his introductions and letters that the demotic could become enriched and molded to serve every literary need. The enemies of the demotic charged that this was an idiom that had developed during the years of barbarism and slavery and that, therefore, it was not fit to be used during the times of freedom and progress. But as Valaoritis had used it, the demotic had achieved a perfect balance of form and content. Such poems as "Thanasis Vayias" and "Astrapoyiannos" were written in a completely appropriate idiom, an idiom in which one would expect the heroes of those poems to speak.[13]

In a later article, published in 1908, Palamas once again touched upon the sensitive topic of the comparison between Solomos and Valaoritis. Here Palamas concedes that the poetry of Valaoritis suffers from the defects of the Romantic poets of his time, but he asks the reader to look beyond the surface, into the more essential elements of Valaoritis' poetry. It is true, Palamas admits, that Valaoritis failed to see Solomos in his true dimensions; his judgment of him,[14] made at a moment of "weakness and egotism," is certainly erroneous. But Valaoritis' intellectual makeup was different from that of Solomos and one can understand why he failed to appreciate him. Valaoritis understood the "external" Solomos, not the "transcendental" one.[15] But had Solomos lived, would he have understood the character and poetic temperament of the bard from Lefkas? One could doubt that. To quote Palamas:

When one reads Solomos for the first time, one forgets about Valaoritis. Then the mind matures. You read Valaoritis again and you see that Solomos does not make him superfluous. You find in him what you did not find in the other: the poetry of detail and of pictorial realism, which, no matter how unpolished, grabs you with its powerful tone. And you put him side by side with the great one, in the place he deserves.[16]

To strengthen his case, Palamas quotes the words of John Psycharis, one of Greece's leading demoticists of the twentieth century: "As great as Solomos is, so great is Valaoritis. Both of them are our fathers; both are children of the same mother, our popular Muse."[17] Palamas finds this judgment useful, but adds the following distinction between the two poets:

The popular Muse, passing through the poetry of Solomos, as if through a magician's garden, becomes a fairy, metaphysical and aristocratic. But when she passes through the poetry of Valaoritis, as if through the fighters' haunts, no matter how she grows and bedecks herself with ornaments, she always remains a chieftainness, positive and democratic.[18]

And again:

The great popular and social meaning of the art of Valaoritis is narrow in its finely wrought, and, incomparable in this, knowledge of every detail of the natural world, contrary to the profound generalities of Solomos.[19]

In a letter titled "Confessions and Faith," published in *Estia*, November 22, 1910, Palamas makes the following points in defense of Valaoritis against hostile criticism:

1. The poetry of Valaoritis is "the most solid" in modern Greek tradition.
2. The language of Valaoritis is the richest language that any poet freed from the shackles of *logiotatismos* (archaism) has used yet.
3. Valaoritis ... is the first pure, and in many ways incomparable, *epic* poet of the new Greek literature.
4. Valaoritis, simple in his manners and even humorous occasionally, is a Homeric poet, a minstrel. Though half-ignored and poorly studied by many Greek critics, he is a poet through and through, a great poet.

On December 12, 1910, Palamas delivered a speech to the
Educational Club, in Athens, comparing Valaoritis to Laskaratos,
the controversial poet and satirist from the island of Cephalonia.
Both men, Palamas argues, made essential contributions to the
development and recognition of Greece's living language. Laskaratos, a rather inept poet, contributed mainly to the development
of prose, in which he used to write all his works. Basically a
prose writer, Laskaratos "never drank from the cup of beauty
and, if he did, he never became drunk."[20] He was "a moralist
rather than a poet, a satirist more than a moralist; poetry for
him was a means to a useful end. . . ."[21] There was no lyricism
in Laskaratos, for his poetry was "a Lucianic jeer, Voltairic
malice, an echo of past Italian times; he was transplanted here,
was original, alive, full of color and character."[22] Laskaratos
himself wrote: "I desired to climb Parnassus, but always halfway
through the rising path I was tired and turned back. I did not
have the wings of my friend Valaoritis."[23]

By contrast, the personality of Valaoritis follows the social
path. The latter is grandoise, optimistic, always engaged in
patriotic struggles. Laskaratos, living most of his life in isolation,
was bitter, vitriolic in his attacks against the clergy, antisocial.
Valaoritis burst out in lyrical exclamations; Laskaratos let off
steam by weaving ironic and poisonous epigrams. "Valaoritis,"
Palamas writes, "was a poet, sociable, fond of politics, a
rhetorician; Laskaratos, on the other hand, was a libeller, always
looking for trouble, antisocial, polemical, a heretic."[24] Laskaratos,
who held an extensive correspondence with the poet from Lefkas,
looked askance at the latter's political activities, complaining
that Valaoritis was wasting too much time away from the call
of his muse. "A long epic poem," he wrote, "would have made
Valaoritis immortal." But Laskaratos failed to see that Valaoritis
served the same aims with his poetry as with his political
activities. Just as Laskaratos served his country with his criticism of the narrow dogmatism and backwardness of the Greek
provincial clergy, so Valaoritis served his nation's interests by
staying in the arena of politics for as long as he did, and by
means of literature. At any rate, Palamas argues in a later
article, Valaoritis did indeed write the equivalent of a national

epic—his entire poetic production, if pieced together, comprises such a whole.[25]

Palamas wrote numerous other articles on the work of Valaoritis in the course of his career. Two speeches delivered to the Educational Club in 1914 represent his most comprehensive analysis of Valaoritis and his work. Some of the most pertinent of his remarks on the longer poems of Valaoritis have already been cited elsewhere.[26] Of the remaining comments, a few are illuminating. Valaoritis, says Palamas, is not a lyric poet; there is no personal confession in his poetry, no sign of personal life to show us that he passed moments of sadness, boredom, pain, ecstasy. His song is not the monologue of a man careless of whether he is being heard; he is not in an ecstatic musical delirium; he does not lean forward to count his heartbeats; he does not lift his eyes to the eternal universal problems. With all the beauty of its natural descriptions, his poetry does not possess the mystic revelation of the soul of man. Neither is it moved by that Dionysian drunkenness that dances and pours forth. Valaoritis does not tumble down into the nihilism of the lyric poet, who "falls into his subject and drowns in it."[27] The object, not the subject, is the main concern of Valaoritis. When, at certain moments, he presents himself in a somewhat lyrical, pindaric, or sapphic mood, he is not his real self. He is not then at his best, he tires easily, and his poetry does not stand comparison.

Valaoritis, for Palamas, is an epic poet so absorbed in the objective representation of his idea that even his shorter poems with a lyrical disposition are small epic pieces. His poems are not confessions, they are stories; they are not hymns, they are tales; they are not monologues, they are dialogues. Such poems as "The Rock and the Wave," "The Bell," "The Wild Vine" are examples of this kind of poetry. Only two of his poems portray love: *Kyra Phrosyni*, with the description of Ali's love for Phrosyni; and *Photeinos*, with the idyll between Thodoula and Lambros. But in both cases the love theme is incidental and a part of a larger context.

Although Valaoritis grew philosophical and became pre-occupied with the theme of death toward the end of his career, Palamas feels that his gamut was national history, Greek nature,

the depiction of the people's customs, habits, and traits. Valaoritis paints; his artistry consists of two elements—a heart and
a picture; he paints the tapestry of Greek nature even in his
saddest moments. His ability to describe and depict nature is
perhaps a means of redemption. Valaoritis is a man who lives
in the open air, who sees and who knows, a nature lover and
a poet. "We can hardly find a poet in our modern literature
who can compare with him in his knowledge of colorful natural
facts and their detailed description," Palamas says.[28] We must
travel far, to Homer and Hesiod, to Theocritus and Virgil, to
find comparable examples. The descriptive power of Valaoritis,
vague and mediocre at first, grows and reaches its peak as his
technique matures. Description becomes more accurate, clearer
and leans heavily on detail.

Valaoritis knows not only Greek nature, but also man and
his environment. He is well acquainted with the language, habits,
domestic items, weapons, dress of the people he talks about,
and his descriptions are "beautifully given in poetic materialism."[29] Scenes of horror are given in raw detail, and the tortures
of heroes are described with exceptional realism. With a force
often approaching that of Dante, he represents the underworld
and the tortures of hell. In all his poems the individual details
are cast against a larger frame: "He represents the man, the
hero who fights, who is tortured and dies guided by the spirit
of liberty; the hero who symbolizes the Greek nation in its
struggle against oppression and slavery."[30]

II   Other Critics

Emmanuel Roidis had known Valaoritis as a man, had spoken
about his work in public,[31] and had corresponded with him
throughout 1878. Immediately after the poet's death in 1879,
Roidis attempted the assessment of his work in an article published in *Estia*, on September 2. In spite of the high esteem in
which Roidis held Valaoritis, he found that the latter had
failed in his mission both as a poet and politician. Valaoritis
had been unable to say, like Horace, *exegi monumentum*, "I have
reared a monument." The political man was unable to win the
victory against corruption, whereas the poet failed to establish a

meaningful relationship with his generation. Valaoritis had failed because he turned to the "antiquated events of the past" to find an ideal, ignoring the realities of the present. Instead of constantly being reminded of the sacrifices of their fore-fathers, the Greeks should rather concentrate on building their homes and securing their present freedoms, Roidis thought.[32] By insisting that the life of the mountaineer klephts had meaning and relevance to the Greek of his day, Valaoritis had "closed his eyes," showing himself out of touch with reality.

But Roidis admired many aspects of the poetry of Valaoritis, especially the richness of his imagination. Reading the poetry of Valaoritis is, as Roidis puts it, "like a ride on winged Pegasus; the scenes change fast, and the rider enjoys fascinating varieties of the landscape." "Most of the descriptions of Valaoritis," Roidis continues in another passage, "resemble neither reliefs, as those of the classical poets, nor a familiar type of painting, but rather a beautiful landscape trembling in the waters of a clear but rarely still lake."[33] The images of Valaoritis produce vivid and unusual sensations; through the expert use of the demotic, the poet achieves genuine sound effects, impossible to render with the purist. Though Valaoritis shares with the Romantic poets of his time the flaw of exaggeration, the clarity of his images and the force of his inspiration outweigh this defect. Valaoritis is the poet of power rather than of perfection, a *megalostomos aidos*, "the singer with the loud voice."

One of the great admirers of Valaoritis in the twentieth century is Paul Nivanas, a fiction writer, journalist, and critic of note. In a speech delivered to the literary club "Parnassus" in Athens (1916), Nirvanas contested the thesis of Palamas that Valaoritis was a par excellence epic poet. The deeper essence of the poetry of Valaoritis, Nirvanas claims, is its lyricism. True, Nirvanas admits, Valaoritis does not seem to be a subjective poet and rarely uses the first person singular. But this does not prevent his poems from being essentially lyrical; lyricism is the expression of personal feeling, a "spontaneous overflow" of emotion, a confession of one heart to another. Though the narrative poems of Valaoritis seem to be of epic character, one cannot miss observing that all his heroes speak his language and use his gesture; his heroes wear the mask of the original; behind the mask is Valaoritis himself; his personality is dormant under the guise of the hero; it is broken up into blocks and lent to each one of his heroes. His heroes "are Valaoritis himself multiplied and transformed into a many-sided lyric impersonation."[34] That is why Valaoritis' characters lack personal, individual psychological traits—they have no features of their own. This is a flaw that Valaoritis shares with many other Romantic poets, Byron in particular. Byron's Childe Harold, Lara, Giaour, Manfred, Sardanapalus, and Cain are all the same character under a different coat. If Valaoritis is an epic poet, he must, like Byron, be "the epic poet of the heart."[35]

Of other twentieth-century critics, several pointed out the pedagogical value of the poetry of Valaoritis. Kostas Varnalis, writing in 1915, claimed that the patriotic themes, the descriptive character of the poetry of Valaoritis, and its close proximity to the folksongs, make it particularly suitable material for school textbooks. Both Theodoros Xydis and Aristos Kambanis—not to mention Palamas—find the poetry of Valaoritis capable of instilling not only feelings of love and devotion for one's own country, but also virtues specifically suited for the molding of character.[36] Xydis points out that since 1884 the poems of Valaoritis have occupied substantial sections in the textbooks of Greek schools. Kambanis finds the poems of Valaoritis, with their richness of language, the best possible source for the study of Modern Greek.[37] Professor Spiros Marinatos recommends that the poems of Valaoritis be used as school textbooks; and Professor G. P. Savidis has clearly demonstrated, in his recent edition of *Photeinos*, that the close study of this poem's text can yield rich fruits.[38] In fact, many poems of Valaoritis, especially the above mentioned, must be studied patiently, with the use of a glossary, if one is to savor the richness and depth of their descriptions and character.

Some of the hostile critics of Valaoritis, who have damaged his reputation and retarded the definitive study of his work, must be mentioned here. Perhaps the most notorious of them is John Apostolakis who, in his book *Aristotelis Valaoritis* (1936), "mobilized all his forces to throw Valaoritis off his pedestal,"[39] as a commentator has put it. Apostolakis attacked Valaoritis "for the absence of Form from his soul."[40] Valaoritis never attempted to present the fighters for freedom "in their total being," never depicted them as they were as men; he only gave their picture partially, presenting only the hero, the fighter for freedom and not the man. "In other words," Apostolakis continues, "Valaoritis was inspired by the idea that the action of the fighter symbolized, and not by the Form of man."[41] His motives were political, and the composition of his poetry was part of a political act and not artistic in origin.

Another hostile critic is Kleon Paraschos, who published numerous articles on Valaoritis in Athens newspapers and periodicals between 1924 and 1938. "Was he a poet? I wonder," Paraschos asks in one of these articles,[42] "or did he transfer into verse his inner romantic disposition?" Every advanced reader of Valaoritis must no doubt put this question to himself. For if Valaoritis is to be judged strictly as an artist, "he is to be found mostly beyond art, outside its scope and meaning." Valaoritis is not a lyrical poet, because he remains silent about man's innermost being. "A fruit sprung from the bowels of the motherland," Paraschos says in a later passage, "part and parcel of Greece, a self-sustained force, full of mountain aromas, Valaoritis did not taste the withering of the men of the city—but neither did he taste their sad, anguished grandeur."[43] I. M. Panayotopoulos, one of Greece's leading critics and men of letters, also finds Valaoritis' poetry wanting, especially when compared to that of Solomos. But Panayotopoulos draws distinctions between the two poets more accurately than many other critics. Solomos, Panayotopoulos claims, cultivated the "feminine elements" of the demotic, while Valaoritis cultivated "the masculine." Valaoritis, in fact, is a nature altogether masculine; he is an excitable, torrential poet who sought to resurrect the heroes of the Greek Revolution and to sing their sacrifices. "He knows nothing of patient craftsmanship of the verse. He is not a craftsman binding gold rings in emerald stone; he is a titan, rolling broken rocks from their tall peaks."[44]

Pointing further differences between Valaoritis and Solomos, Panayotopoulos says that while Solomos "achieves his heroism *in the poem,* Valaoritis expresses it *with the poem.*" This difference is very important. Solomos loves the smooth surfaces and works hard to refine his lines to perfection; Valaoritis piles unhewn stones one upon another. A reader must have a limited artistic and aesthetic consciousness to enjoy him. But Valaoritis has his good qualities also. Poems such as "The Escape" and "Astrapoyiannos" have force, power, and evoke the feeling of a nightmare; the second poem even touches us, and we hear in it a cry from the human heart.[45]

It is difficult to assess the achievement of Valaoritis, especially if one cannot read him in the original, from as diverse critical opinions as have been shown here. The above is, in fact, only a small segment—hopefully representative—of what Greek critics have written on Valaoritis. It is important that, in assessing his achievement, one understands his limitations. Valaoritis was a product of the Romantic era and, in spite of the fact that he consciously fought to shake off its influence, he inherited the flaws of rhetorism, exaggeration, pomposity. He seemed to prefer subjects for his poems that have little intellectual content. He spoke in a loud voice, a mode of expression that went out of fashion with the advent of Cavafy, Seferis, and the other twentieth-century Greek poets who have dominated the scene of Greek letters in recent decades. Perhaps, his poetry is offensive to certain kinds of readers whose sensibility has been shaped by the poets of nuance, symbolism, introspection. But Valaoritis cannot, for these, or any other, reasons, be eliminated. The fact remains that he continues to be popular. "He is a poet that has endured," writes Nikos Pappas. "And a place belongs to him in modern Greek literature, not only because of his popularity, but because there must be 'something else' hidden inside his writings; something that continues to bring him in touch with the hearts of Greeks."[46]

But Valaoritis should be studied for other reasons as well: he is a representative of the first stage, the formative period of Greek literature after the War of Independence, and an important link between the poets of the Heptanese and those of Athens. To understand him one must see him as poet in his own right, rather than as a rival of Solomos—the constant comparison of the two poets on dissimilar grounds is simply fruitless. The two men were different in personality, character, and poetic consciousness. But as one came after the other, and as both belonged to the same school of poetry, one could perhaps best see the two not as rivals but as the successive stages in the development of Greek literature. To use the words of G. P. Savidis, one could regard Solomos as the poet "who built roads," while Valaoritis "built the bridges" for others to follow—Palamas, Sikelianos, and Seferis.[47] This image sharply defines the role that Valaoritis played in the literature of his young nation. But one must recall that Valaoritis was not only a poet, but a man who became involved in all the agonizing problems of his time. He saw that Greece needed internal coherence, a viable political system, an awareness of the sacrifices and heroism of the past, a noble vision for the future. As a poet, political leader, folklorist, courtier, historian, and simply as a man, he contributed to the above aims as much as any man of his times, in a manner all his own, with the writing of poetry that has a unique appeal to the imagination and heart of Greece.

Notes and References

1. Besides Solomos and Valaoritis, other poets, such as Achilles Paraschos, George Zalokostas, and Lorenzo Mavillis, have been considered as national poets. See Stephanos Dafnis, quoted in B. D. Patriarcheas, ed., *Aristotelis Valaoritis* (Athens, 1955), p. 58.

2. C. A. Trypanis, "Greek Literature Since the Fall of Constantinople in 1453," in *The Balkans in Transition*, edited by Charles and Barbara Jelavich (Berkeley and Los Angeles, 1963), p. 229.

3. See K. T. Dimaras, *A History of Modern Literature* (Athens, 1948), p. 177.

4. *Ibid.*, p. 178.

5. *Ibid.*, p. 19–20.

6. *Ibid.*, p. 20. See also Kimon Friar, *Modern Greek Poetry* (New York, 1973), p. 9, and Trypanis, p. 238.

7. Dimaras, p. 244.

8. *Ibid.*, p. 175.

9. *Ibid.*, p. 234.

10. *Ibid.*, p. 239.

11. See "Preface to *Kyra Phrosyni*," in *Aristotelis Valaoritis, Life and Works,* 3 vols., edited by John Valaoritis (Athens, 1908), vol. III, p. 16. Also "Preface to *Athanasis Diakos*," *Ibid.*, vol. III, p. 165. References to the above volumes from here on will be indicated as Maraslis I, II, or III.

12. "Verses written on the Day before my Departure for Switzerland," a youthful poem, is modeled after Byron's *Childe Harold*. See Patriarcheas, p. 35.

13. Letter to Emmanuel Roidis, November 3, 1877. Maraslis I, p. 221.

14. *Ibid.*, p. 220.

15. *Ibid.*, p. 218.

16. Translation of "The Lake," in Maraslis I, pp. 234–37.

17. Maraslis II, pp. 52–61.

18. "Ode to Patriarch Gregorios V," in particular.

19. Ten idylls were translated, among which are "The Cyclops," "To the Dead Adonis," and "Thyrsis." For analysis and comments

159

of the translations, see *Unpublished Poems,* edited by B. D. Patriarcheas (Athens, 1937), pp. 89–136.

20. See Letter to Andreas Laskaratos, October 3, 1859, Maraslis I, p. 519.

21. Aristos Kambanis, "Preface" to *Complete Works,* vol. I (Athens, 1961), p. 15.

22. Dimaras, p. 314.

23. For an illustration of this practice, see Letter to Laskaratos, May 12, 1859, Maraslis I, p. 514.

24. A Letter to Aimilios Typaldos, used as "Preface" to *Mnemosyna,* Maraslis I, p. 37.

25. See "Preface to *Kyra Prosyni,*" Maraslis III, p. 7.

26. Preface to *Athanasis Diakos,*" Maraslis III, pp. 165–66.

27. "Poetic materialism" is the term Palamas coined to signify the concreteness of imagery in the poetry of Valaoritis. See Kostis Palamas, *Aristotelis Valaoritis* (Athens, 1924), p. 116.

28. Kostis Palamas, "Aristotelis Valaoritis," reprinted from the periodical *Estia,* Maraslis I, p. 311.

29. See above mentioned Letter to Roidis, Maraslis I, p. 225.

30. Maraslis I, p. 276.

31. "On the Death of Andonios Kondaris," a poem sent to the young man's father as a letter of condolence, Maraslis II, p. 227.

Chapter Two

1. Maraslis I, p. 4.

2. *Ibid.*

3. *Ibid.,* p. 15.

4. Reference is made here to the poems discovered by B. D. Patriarcheas in 1937. See *Unpublished Poems,* pp. 89–136.

5. Stephanos Koumanoudis, a noted critic of his time.

6. Pen name for Helen Gicas-Kotsou Massalsky, a Rumanian-born critic, who wrote for both the Italian and French presses. She corresponded with Valaoritis and contributed articles that made him known to European audiences. See Gerasimos Grigoris, *Aristotelis Valaoritis; Life, Works, A Critical Anthology with Pictures* (Athens, 1975), p. 142.

7. Maraslis I, p. 82.

8. *Ibid.,* p. 137.

9. Emmanuel Roidis, "Aristotelis Valaoritis," reprinted from *Estia,* September 2, 1879, in Maraslis I, p. 303.

10. "Valaoritis as a Politician," in Palamas, *Aristotelis Valaoritis,* chapter 9, p. 130.

11. Maraslis I, p. 276.

12. Reference is made to the creation of "Greater Bulgaria" by the Treaty of San Stepfano, 1877.

13. Maraslis I, p. 276.

14. *Ibid.*, p. 278.

Chapter Three

1. The story of the discovery is told in detail in *Unpublished Poems*, pp. 3–39.

2. See Chapter Two, pp. 00–00.

3. See *Unpublished Poems*, pp. 17–19.

4. Patriarcheas, pp. 26–40.

5. Kleon Paraschos, *Nea Estia*, vol. 254. Reprinted in *ibid.*, pp. 60–61.

6. Maraslis II, p. 36.

7. *Ibid.*, p. 37.

8. *Ibid.*, pp. 51–52.

9. *Ibid.* The massacre of the population of Gardiki and the role of Vayias in it are vividly described by George Finlay, *History of the Greek Revolution* (1877; reprinted London, 1971), vol. I, p. 67.

10. Reference is to Rhigas Pheraios. For details, see Chapter One, pp. 00–00.

11. Maraslis II, p. 101.

12. Palamas, *Aristotelis Valaoritis*, p. 67.

13. *Ibid.*, p. 68.

Chapter Four

1. See his "Preface to *Kyra Phrosyni*," Maraslis III, p. 8.

2. See John Valaoritis, "Biographical Notes," Maraslis I, p. 56.

3. Maraslis III, pp. 23–118.

4. Letter to Laskaratos, October 3, 1859, Maraslis I, p. 519.

5. *Ibid.*

6. *Ibid.*

7. Maraslis III, p. 8.

8. *Ibid.*

9. *Ibid.*

10. For further information on the subject, see Finlay, p. 60.

11. Maraslis III, p. 14.

12. *Ibid.*

13. Maraslis I, p. 56.

14. *Ibid.*, p. 518.

15. *Ibid.*, p. 302.

16. Angelos Sikelianos, "Aristotelis Valaoritis" (Speech delivered to an audience in Athens in 1943), in *Complete Works* (ed. Tavoularis) (Athens, 1966), p. 12.

17. Kambanis, p. 8.

18. Dimaras, p. 316.

19. Paul Nirvanas, "A Speech on Valaoritis" (given to an audience in Athens in 1916), *Elliniki Dimiourgia*, vol. IV (Athens, July 15, 1949), p. 107.

20. Palamas, *Aristotelis Valaoritis*, p. 70.

21. *Ibid.*

22. Maraslis I, p. 115.

23. *Ibid.*, p. 126.

24. Roidis, p. 303.

25. Maraslis III, p. 171.

26. *Ibid.*

27. *Ibid.*, p. 172.

28. Maraslis I, p. 116.

29. Maraslis III, pp. 165–66.

30. Palamas, *Aristotelis Valaoritis*, p. 101.

31. Maraslis III, pp. 167–68.

32. *Ibid.*

33. *Ibid.*, p. 153.

34. Maraslis I, p. 111.

35. Maraslis III, p. 170.

36. *Ibid.*

37. Palamas, "Aristotelis Valaoritis," Maraslis I, p. 319.

38. *Ibid.*

39. *Ibid.*, p. 322.

40. *Ibid.*

41. *Ibid.*, p. 324.

42. *Ibid.*

43. "First Speech," given before an audience in the Educational Club, January 8, 1914. See Palamas, *Aristotelis Valaoritis*, pp. 73–78.

44. Nirvanas, p. 108.

45. Dimaras, p. 316.

46. Sikelianos, p. 12.

47. Kambanis, p. 11.

48. Spiros Melas, "Aristotelis Valaoritis, the Singer of the Country," *Elliniki Dimiourgia*, vol. IV (Athens, July 15, 1949), p. 86.

49. Nirvanas, p. 108.

Chapter Five

1. Palamas, *Aristotelis Valaoritis*, p. 110.
2. The poetry of Hugo and Lamartine in particular.
3. Maraslis II, p. 126.
4. Dimaras, p. 319.
5. Nirvanas, p. 110.
6. I. M. Panayotopoulos, *Writers and Their Works*, vol. IV, *The Greek and the Foreign* (Athens, 1950), p. 79.
7. Sikelianos, p. 12.
8. Palamas, *Aristotelis Valaoritis*, p. 80.
9. Maraslis III, pp. 268–69.
10. Palamas, *Aristotelis Valaoritis*, p. 80.
11. Poetic rendition by Robert Stanton.
12. Grigoris, p. 90.

Chapter Six

1. "Preface to *Kyra Phrosyni*," Maraslis III, p. 8.
2. Maraslis III, pp. 327–39.
3. Palamas, *Aristotelis Valaoritis*, p. 82.
4. Maraslis I, p. 272.
5. *Ibid.*, p. 274.
6. *Ibid.*, p. 273.
7. Roidis never mentions *Photeinos* in his article of 1879.
8. Maraslis I, p. 273.
9. Palamas, *Aristotelis Valaoritis*, p. 82.
10. *Ibid.*
11. *Ibid.*, p. 85.
12. *Ibid.*, p. 89.
13. *Ibid.*
14. *Ibid.*, p. 90.
15. Melas, p. 85.
16. Kambanis, p. 14.
17. Nirvanas, p. 110.
18. *Ibid.*
19. Sikelianos, p. 13.
20. *Ibid.*
21. *Ibid.*, p. 14.
22. *Ibid.*, p. 15.

Chapter Seven

1. Quoted by Theodoros Xydis, in Grigoris, p. 154.

2. "Solomos and Valaoritis," in Palamas, *Aristotelis Valaoritis,* chapter 3, p. 19.

3. Dimaras, pp. 317–18.

4. *Ibid.,* p. 319.

5. See G. P. Savidis, *Aristotelis Valaoritis: Photeinos* (Athens, 1973), p. 10.

6. See Chapter Two, p. 00.

7. Dimaras, pp. 318–19; and Savidis, pp. 9–10.

8. See discussions in Chapter Four, pp. 00–00.

9. To my knowledge, the exceptions to this rule are *Unpublished Poems* (1937), edited by B. D. Patriarcheas, and G. P. Savidis' edition of *Photeinos* (1970).

10. Palamas, "Aristotelis Valaoritis," Maraslis I, p. 306.

11. *Ibid.,* p. 308.

12. *Ibid.*

13. *Ibid.,* p. 311.

14. Palamas, *Aristotelis Valaoritis,* p. 18.

15. *Ibid.*

16. *Ibid.,* p. 19.

17. *Ibid.,* p. 20.

18. *Ibid.*

19. *Ibid.,* p. 21.

20. *Ibid.,* p. 31.

21. *Ibid.*

22. *Ibid.*

23. *Ibid.,* p. 32.

24. *Ibid.,* p. 33.

25. *Ibid.,* p. 101.

26. See discussions in Chapter Four, pp. 00–00.

27. Palamas, *Aristotelis Valaoritis,* p. 102.

28. *Ibid.,* p. 103.

29. *Ibid.,* p. 115.

30. *Ibid.,* p. 116.

31. Reference is made to a speech delivered by Roidis to the club Parnassus, Athens, October 1877. The text of the speech was sent to Valaoritis, and this sparked off the correspondence between the two men which lasted until January 1878.

32. Maraslis I, p. 294.

33. *Ibid.,* p. 296.

34. Nirvanas, p. 107.

35. *Ibid.*

36. Kambanis, p. 11; Theodoros Xydis, in Grigoris, p. 165.

37. Kambanis, p. 15.

38. Marinatos, "Aristotelis Valaoritis as a Man and a Poet," *Elliniki Dimiourgia*, vol. IV (Athens, July 15, 1949), p. 91; "Photeinos for us Today," in Savidis, pp. 9–67.

39. Grigoris, p. 150.

40. *Ibid.*

41. *Ibid.*

42. An article appearing in the newspaper *Dimokratia*, June 7, 1925.

43. *Ibid.*

44. Panayotopoulos, p. 79.

45. *Ibid.*, p. 80.

46. Quoted in Grigoris, p. 154.

47. Savidis, p. 10.

Selected Bibliography

PRIMARY SOURCES

Life and Works. 3 vols. Edited by John Valaoritis [the son of the poet]. Athens: Maraslis Library, 1908. These volumes contain all the known works by Valaoritis up to that time, a biography of the poet, a considerable portion of his correspondence, and early critical studies. I have used this edition as my basic text.

Unpublished Poems. Edited with an introduction by Vasilios D. Patriarcheas. Athens: John Kollaros, 1937. Poems written during Valaoritis' youth were brought forth as new material unknown until 1937 by this scholar.

Complete Works. 2 vols. Edited with a preface by Aristos Kambanis. Athens: Philologiki, 1961.

Complete Works. 1 vol. Edited by S. Tavoularis, with a preface by Angelos Sikelianos. Athens: Greek Publishing Company, 1966.

Complete Works. 2 vols. Edited by John Koutsoglou, with an Introduction by B. D. Patriarcheas. Athens: Greek Publishing Company, 1967.

SECONDARY SOURCES

1. Criticism and Secondary Material

APOSTOLAKIS, JOHN. *Aristotelis Valaoritis.* Athens, 1936. The work of Valaoritis is examined as a whole, from a literary and aesthetic point of view. Apostolakis, who is an ardent follower of Solomos, finds too many flaws in the poetry of Valaoritis, and his criticism is patently biased.

KAMBANIS, ARISTOS. "Preface." In *Complete Works*, edited by Aristos Kambanis. Athens: Philologiki, 1961. The article is facile and oversimplifies many issues, but it strongly points out the contributions of Valaoritis to the question of language.

MARINATOS, SPIROS. "Aristotelis Valaoritis, the Man and the Poet." *Elliniki Dimiourgia.* Vol. IV. Athens, July 15, 1949. Hardly scholarly, the essay of Professor Marinatos attempts to evaluate Valaoritis as a man and patriot, offering suggestions why the poetry of Valaoritis is relevant to the problems of modern youth. The didactic value of the works of Valaoritis is pointed out.

MELAS, SPIROS. "Aristotelis Valaoritis, the Singer of the Country," *Elliniki Dimiourgia*. Vol. IV. Athens, July 15, 1949. Strong support is given Valaoritis by Melas, though the article as a whole is overenthusiastic and rhapsodic in tone.

NIRVANAS, PAUL. "A Speech on Valaoritis." *Elliniki Dimiourgia*. Vol. IV. Athens, July 15, 1949. A valuable essay; it examines the question of the Greek epic in its relation to the poetry of Valaoritis. An excellent brief analysis is given of principal poems.

PALAMAS, KOSTIS. *Aristotelis Valaoritis; 1824–1924; Articles, Letters, Speeches*. Athens: Eleftheroudiakis, 1924. This slender volume contains most of the significant articles of Palamas on Valaoritis, and it is an indispensable tool for the study of the poet.

PANAYOTOPOULOS, I. M. *Writers and Their Works*. Vol. IV, *The Greek and the Foreign*. Athens: John Kollaros, 1950. Among numerous articles on Greek and non-Greek authors, one of the most insightful is "The Greek Romanticism," in the section on poetry. The comparison between Solomos and Valaoritis is here fruitful, especially the comments on the style and poetic temperament of the two men.

PARASCHOS, KLEON. "Aristotelis Valaoritis; a Hundred Years." An article in the newspaper *Dimokratia*, June 7, 1925. The most forcefully written adverse criticism of Valaoritis, strange in view of the fact that Paraschos wrote numerous other articles on Valaoritis on the whole favorable and objective.

PATRIARCHEAS, B. D., ed. *Aristotelis Valaoritis Speaks Against the English Occupation*. Athens, 1955 (no publisher quoted). The edition of a hitherto unpublished poem, "The Last Day Before my Departure for Switzerland," is given here for the first time. Valuable critical comments by many Greek scholars upon the publication of *Unpublished Poems* in 1937 are included. The poem and its background are analyzed.

ROIDIS, EMMANUEL. "Aristotelis Valaoritis." An article published in *Estia*, September 2, 1889; reprinted in *Life and Works*, edited by John Valaoritis. Athens: Maraslis Library, 1908. One of the earliest and most important critical articles on the work of Valaoritis as a whole. Keen critical observations and analyses of major poems with the exception *Photeinos*. The attitude of Roidis is on the whole favorable, but he strongly supports the view that Valaoritis failed to relate as a poet to the climate of his own generation.

SAVIDIS, G. P. *Aristotelis Valaoritis; Photeinos*. Athens: New Greek Library, Hermes Editions, 1970. The most scholarly and critically

astute edition of the major poem *Photeinos*. It sets forth the
model to follow in further critical editions of the remaining
works of Valaoritis.

SIKELIANOS, ANGELOS. "Aristotelis Valaoritis." Speech delivered to
an audience in Athens in 1943. In *Complete Works*, edited by
S. Tavoularis. Athens: Greek Publishing Company, 1966. Sikelianos concentrates on the poet and the man rather than his works.
He writes with his usual rhapsodic fervor, but his analyses of
"Astrapoyiannos" and *Photeinos* are a brilliant addition to Valaoritis criticism.

XYDIS, THEODOROS. "Valaoritis and his Meaning in our Times." An
article published in *New Year's Literature*, 1973. Xydis attempts
briefly to reevaluate the work of Valaoritis and to point out his
relevance to our times. He answers hostile criticism, especially
that of Apostolakis.

2.   General Works

DIMARAS, K. T. *A History of Modern Greek Literature.* Athens:
Ikaros, 1948. (English translation by Mary Gianos, Albany,
New York, 1972.) A monumental work, this is considered the
best history of modern Greek literature, although not all the
treatments of individual authors have depth. A good study is
provided of the origins of modern Greek literature; good treatments of Solomos, Kalvos, Palamas, and Sikelianos. The Valaoritis
section has some good points, but on the whole it is insufficient.

FINLAY, GEORGE. *History of the Greek Revolution.* 2 vols in 1. Oxford:
Clarendon Press, 1877; reprinted, London: Zeno Booksellers
and Publishers, 1971. Though biased, this is considered the best
study of the Greek War of Independence written by a non-Greek
author. Especially good in outlining the background of the
Greek war. A good background for the student of Greek
literature.

FRIAR, KIMON. *Modern Greek Poetry.* New York: Simon and Schuster,
1973. Outstanding translations of modern Greek poets. A chapter
on the craft of Greek poetry is especially valuable to the student
of Greek prosody. A valuable guide for translators.

GRIGORIS, GERASIMOS. *Aristotelis Valaoritis, 1824–1879; Life, Works,
A Critical Anthology with Pictures.* Athens: Company of Lefkas
Studios, 1975. A popular edition, this volume is done with
taste and literary acumen, and is indeed a good combination
of biography, criticism, pictures, and a selection of the poet's

most important works. The bibliographical section is rich and up-to-date.

LAZARIS, CHRISTOPHOROS. *Ta Lefkaditika; an Etymological Dictionary of the Spoken Idioms of Lefkas, with Interpretations.* Jannina, 1970. An excellent, scholarly edition of the idioms, words, and locutions of Lefkas, valuable for the study of the work of Valaoritis.

MASKALERIS, THANASIS. *Kostis Palamas.* New York: Twayne Publishers, 1972. Though Valaoritis is hardly mentioned in this volume, the analysis of the work of Palamas and the assessment of its importance is helpful to the student of the works of Valaoritis. Both poets had a common interest in the establishment of the demotic as the language of literature in Greece.

MARVOKORDATO, JOHN. *Modern Greece; A Chronicle and a Survey; 1800–1931.* London: McMillan and Company, 1931. Though this book is a "history" of modern Greece, sections of it are devoted to a brief but perceptive analysis of principal Greek authors.

NITZE, WILLIAM, and PRESTON E. DARGAN. *A History of French Literature.* 3rd ed. New York: 1958. Offers useful background material in attempting to relate the poetry of Valaoritis to French Romantic authors and to trace their influence on him.

RAIZIS, M. BYRON. *Dionysios Solomos.* New York: Twayne Publishers, 1972. Important insights are offered here into the life of Solomos and its relation to his art. Detailed and scholarly, especially in relating Solomos and his work to the Romantic movement in Europe. The influence of Solomos on Palamas, and other subsequent Greek poets, is well described. Comparisons of Solomos to Valaoritis are rather conventional and unflattering to the latter.

SOLOMOS, DIONYSIOS. *A Commemorative Issue. Nea Estia,* no. 731 (Christmas issue). Athens: 1957. Critical articles on Solomos, a few with reference to Valaoritis, appear in this special volume.

TRYPANIS, C. A. "Greek Literature Since the Fall of Constantinople in 1453." In *The Balkans in Transition,* edited by Charles and Barbara Jelavich. Berkeley and Los Angeles: University of California Press, 1963. This book in general contains several articles pertaining to recent Balkan history. Professor Trypanis' article is a brilliant introduction to the study of modern Greek literature, particularly since it is geared to an English-speaking audience.

Index

171